Somatic Psychotherapy for

HEALING TRAUMA

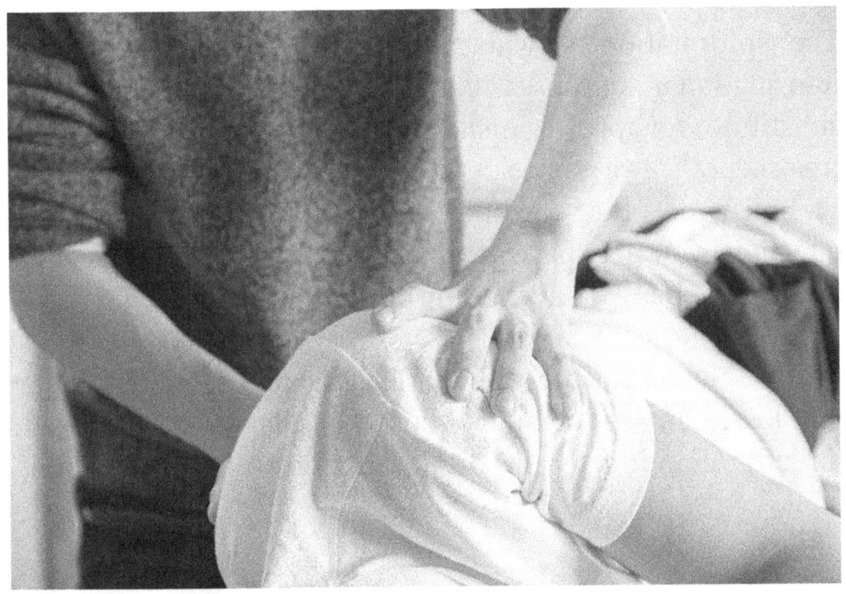

Dr. Deidre Glock

COPYRIGHT

Trademarks:

All trademarks, service marks, and product names mentioned in this book are the property of their respective owners and are used for identification purposes only. Use of these names, trademarks, and brands does not imply endorsement.

Dedication

To GOD

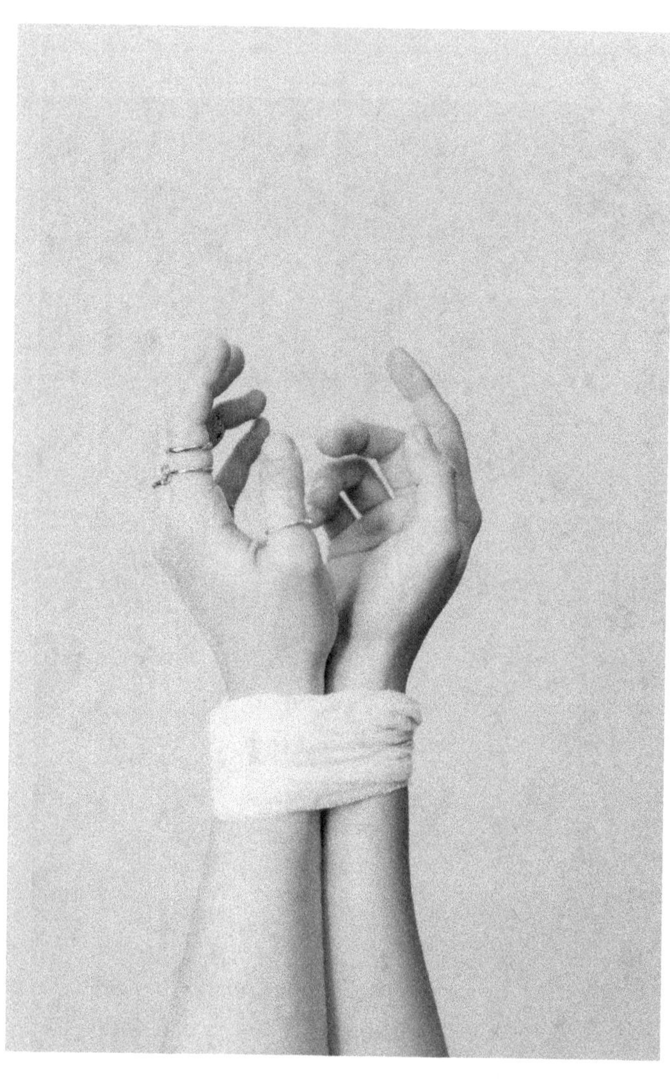

Introduction

There once was a woman named Emily who lived in a cute little town. She could brighten even the darkest room with her smile, but she was hiding serious emotional scars from her past beneath that beautiful exterior. Emily had gone through a horrific event as a child that followed her into adulthood. She made an effort to go on, but the anguish seemed to permeate every part of her life.

Emily had heard about somatic psychotherapy, a comprehensive strategy that emphasized using the body-mind connection to heal trauma. She made the choice to test it out because she was curious and in need of relief. Dr. Turner welcomed Emily with warmth and understanding. He is a skilled and kind somatic therapist.

Dr. Turner gently encouraged Emily to relate her tale during their initial consultation. As she described the incidents that had plagued her for so long, tears began to fall down her cheeks. Dr. Turner listened carefully, recognizing Emily's suffering and praising her for having the bravery to face her history.

Dr. Turner assisted Emily in growing her awareness of her body's sensations and responses as the therapy went on. They found that some memories caused physical reactions like tightness in her chest, stomach knots, or shallow breathing. Emily discovered through somatic psychotherapy that the body frequently retained memories of traumatic events, and these unresolved emotions showed as physical ailments.

Together, they explored Emily's feelings and helped her eventually overcome the trauma. Dr. Turner taught Emily mindfulness practices and urged her to observe her feelings and sensations objectively. She found greater stability through breathing techniques, which also gave her newfound control over her body and emotions.

In one especially enlightening session, Dr. Turner advised using a method known as "body movement exploration." Emily was skeptical at first but ultimately chose to trust the procedure. She let her body to flow naturally, conveying her emotions without using words as soft music played in the background.

Emily was caught off guard dancing, a lovely, flowing movement that seemed to express the indescribable. The movements depicted suffering, but they also showed tenacity and optimism. Dr. Turner was in wonder as he observed Emily's body releasing the constrained emotions to make place for recovery and development.

With time, Emily's development became clear. Her bright smile started to exude true joy and contentment. She no longer considered herself a victim of her past. Instead, she had taken back control of her life and used her newfound strength to rewrite the story of her trauma.

With each session, Emily felt her emotional burden lessen and her compassion for herself grow. Emily had been able to accept the present with open arms and make peace with her past thanks to Dr. Turner's counseling and physical psychotherapy.

Emily's path to recovery was not without obstacles, but armed with the skills she learned in somatic psychotherapy, she overcame them with bravery and tenacity. She came to understand the strength of her body-mind link and her capacity for internal healing.

As the days grew into weeks, then into months, Emily became a ray of hope for other trauma survivors. She discovered that she was drawn to support groups, where she shared her experience to uplift and enthuse those who were still suffering.

On her path to recovery, Emily not only learned about the transforming potential of somatic psychotherapy, but she also realized her calling: assisting others in discovering their own paths to recovery, just as she had. She accepted her vocation to shed light on the lives of others affected by trauma because of her personal experience, and she was aware that this was only the beginning of her incredible narrative.

1.1 Understanding Trauma and its Impact

Trauma is a psychological and emotional reaction to upsetting or upsetting situations that are thought to pose a serious danger to one's life or significantly affect one's wellbeing. Events like physical or sexual assault, natural catastrophes, accidents, conflict, life-threatening sickness, the death of a loved one, or other very upsetting circumstances may all qualify as traumatic experiences. Trauma may have a significant and long-lasting effect on a person's life, negatively impacting their mental, emotional, physical, and social wellbeing.

One of the most well-known psychological repercussions of trauma is the onset of post-traumatic stress disorder (PTSD). People with PTSD may avoid reminders of the traumatic incident, have intrusive and upsetting memories or dreams connected to it, and show hypervigilance or an excessive startle reaction.

- Flashbacks: Despite being in a secure place, trauma survivors may suffer flashbacks during which they feel as if they are reliving the painful incident.

- Emotional Dysregulation: Trauma may result in emotional dysregulation, which can bring on strong and erratic feelings including grief, fear, guilt, and humiliation.

- Dissociation: Some people use this defensive strategy to distance themselves from reality in order to deal with intense emotions.

2. Physical Impact: - Chronic Pain and Physical Health concerns: Trauma has been associated with autoimmune

illnesses, cardiovascular difficulties, and other physical health concerns as well as chronic pain conditions.

- Modified Stress Response: Trauma may alter the body's stress response mechanism, increasing cortisol levels and stress sensitivity.

3. Cognitive Impact: - Memory Issues: Trauma may result in memory and attention issues, making it difficult to concentrate on activities or recall specifics.

Negative self-ideas may result in a gloomy attitude and poor self-esteem in trauma survivors. Trauma survivors may also acquire negative beliefs about other people, the world, and themselves.

4. Social Impact: - Interpersonal Difficulties: Trauma may have an impact on relationships, making it hard to trust others, making you afraid of intimacy, and making it hard to make new friends.

- Social Isolation: As a coping tactic, some trauma survivors avoid social situations, which results in isolation and loneliness.

5. Coping Mechanisms: - Substance Abuse: Some people use alcohol or drugs to ease the emotional agony brought on by trauma.

- Self-Harm: Trauma may cause people to engage in self-destructive activities like self-harm as a method to cope with their emotions or regain control.

6. Long-Term Effects: - Resilience and development: Trauma may be very difficult, but many people exhibit extraordinary resilience and can go through post-traumatic development,

where they get a fresh perspective on life and discover their own inner resources while going through the healing process.

   - Delayed Onset: Some people may not feel the full effects of trauma right once, and symptoms may not show up for months or even years.

Often, professional assistance is needed to address the effects of trauma. Psychotherapy is often used to assist trauma survivors in processing their emotions, changing limiting beliefs, and creating more effective coping mechanisms. Examples include cognitive-behavioral therapy (CBT) and eye movement desensitization and reprocessing (EMDR). When trauma-related symptoms severely impair everyday functioning, medication may be recommended.

The recovery process depends heavily on supportive and understanding relationships, community resources, and a secure environment. The path to trauma recovery may be difficult, but with the correct help and treatments, people can reclaim their feeling of security, value, and hope for the future.

1.2 Overview of Somatic Psychotherapy

A comprehensive therapeutic approach known as somatic psychotherapy acknowledges the inherent interdependence of the mind and body in the healing process. This method sees psychological and emotional problems as physically manifested in a person's motions and experiences. Somatic psychotherapy tries to treat psychological issues at both the cognitive and somatic levels, fostering a deeper understanding and integration of emotions and behaviors by including the body's feelings and sensations into the therapeutic process.

The idea that the body accumulates and conveys emotional and psychological events is at the heart of somatic psychotherapy. These repressed emotions might surface as physical tensions, stances, gestures, and other expressions. Clients and therapists may learn more about the underlying emotional and psychological problems by observing these physical indicators.

The therapeutic paradigms and methods employed in somatic psychotherapy include body psychotherapy, Gestalt therapy, psychodynamic theory, mindfulness techniques, and trauma-focused approaches. Exercises for body awareness, breathing exercises, movement exploration, touch, and methods for physical grounding are typical strategies. To foster emotional healing and self-awareness, the therapist may lead clients in exploring physical sensations, tracking emotions in the body, and encouraging the release of stored tensions.

For those who have had trauma or have trouble vocally expressing their feelings, this treatment is very useful. Somatic psychotherapy provides a safe and gentle technique to address traumatic events and promote resilience by using the body in the therapeutic process.

Key principles and goals of somatic psychotherapy may include:

1. Embodied awareness: Encouraging clients to develop a deeper connection with their physical sensations, emotions, and bodily experiences.

2. Regulation of the nervous system: Helping clients regulate their autonomic nervous system to reduce anxiety, stress, and hyperarousal responses.

3. Release of physical and emotional tension: Facilitating the release of held physical tension and emotional blocks, allowing for greater emotional processing.

4. Integration of body and mind: Recognizing the interconnectedness of body and mind and promoting harmony between the two aspects of the self.

5. Trauma healing: Addressing past trauma by safely processing and integrating traumatic memories at both cognitive and somatic levels.

6. Mindfulness and presence: Cultivating present-moment awareness to enhance self-acceptance and self-compassion.

Somatic psychotherapy is practiced by licensed mental health professionals who have received specialized training in somatic approaches. The therapeutic process may take place in individual, group, or couples/family settings, depending on the client's needs and preferences.

It's important to note that somatic psychotherapy is not a one-size-fits-all approach, and its effectiveness may vary from person to person. Some individuals may find great benefit in combining somatic techniques with other traditional therapeutic modalities, while others may find it more impactful as a standalone approach.

Overall, somatic psychotherapy offers a unique and valuable perspective on healing that recognizes the profound interconnectedness of mind, body, and emotions, providing clients with a holistic pathway to greater self-awareness and well-being.

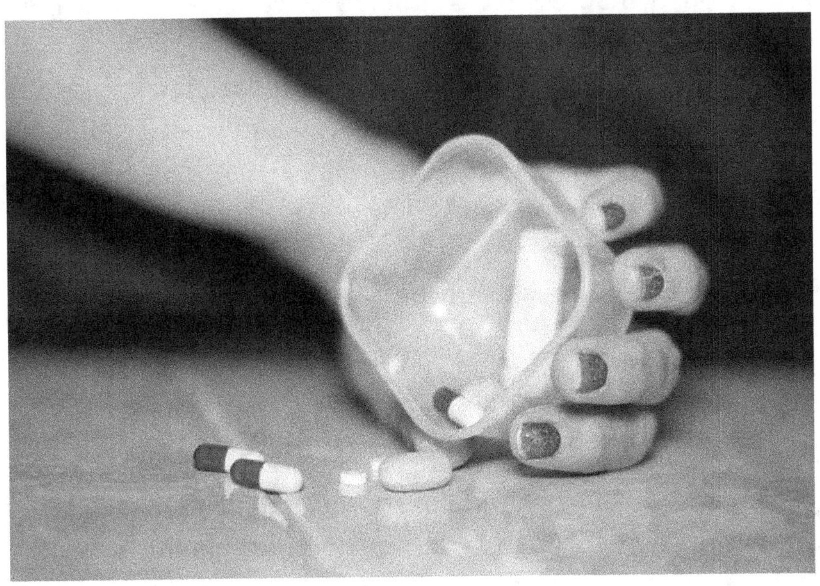

1.3 Importance of Somatic Approaches in Trauma Healing

Somatic methods of trauma recovery have become more important and well-known in the therapeutic and mental health fields. These methods emphasize the mind-body link and acknowledge that trauma is both a psychological and an embodied experience. Somatic therapies are essential for healing trauma for the following main reasons:

1. Examining the Role of the Body in Trauma: Traumatic events are often retained in the body, causing physical tension, pain, and other somatic symptoms. It's possible that conventional talk treatments are insufficient to help people process and release these ingested traumas. On the other side, somatic techniques work directly with the body to relax physical tension and let the nervous system settle, opening up previously inaccessible trauma for access and processing.

2. Restoring Safety and Regulation: Trauma may impair the body's innate capacity for safety and self-regulation. Individuals who use somatic therapies may better control overwhelming emotions and triggers by regaining a feeling of safety in their bodies. The nervous system may be brought into a more balanced condition by using methods including breathing exercises, grounding, and movement.

3. Empowerment and Agency: Somatic treatments enable patients to actively participate in their recovery. Individuals get a feeling of agency and control over their experiences by increasing their awareness of body sensations and learning strategies to deal with them. For trauma survivors to reclaim

a feeling of command over their life after going through terrible experiences, this empowerment is crucial.

4. Traumatic events may be preverbal or nonverbal in form, particularly those that take place early in life. This implies that accessing the memories and effects of trauma via conventional conversation therapy may not be simple. Through body-based procedures, somatic therapies provide a way to access and manage these nonverbal components of trauma.

5. Integration of Mind and Body: Trauma may cause a rift between the mind and body, resulting in feelings of emotional numbness and dissociation. These elements are intended to be integrated via somatic techniques, which encourage a feeling of greater completeness and self-awareness. People may better comprehend and deal with the emotional and psychological impacts of trauma as they grow more attuned to their bodies.

6. Trauma-Informed Care: Many trauma survivors have had negative experiences in conventional mental health institutions, where the main emphasis is on linguistic and cognitive functioning. A safer and more sensitive therapy setting that recognizes the effects of trauma on the body and mind is created by somatic techniques, which place an emphasis on trauma-informed treatment.

7. Long-Term and Complete Healing: Somatic treatments may supplement conventional talk therapies and improve the efficacy of trauma therapy. These methods provide a more thorough and long-lasting healing process by

addressing both the psychological and physiological elements of trauma.

Since trauma affects the whole individual, somatic therapies for healing trauma understand the intricate connection between the mind and body. People have a better chance of processing, healing, and eventually recovering from traumatic events when body-based strategies are used in trauma treatment.

Theoretical Foundations of Somatic Psychotherapy

Somatic psychotherapy is a branch of therapy that focuses on the integration of the mind and body in the healing process. It is based on the fundamental belief that the body holds valuable insights, wisdom, and untapped potential for emotional and psychological growth. This approach recognizes that the mind and body are interconnected, influencing each other in profound ways. The theoretical foundations of somatic psychotherapy draw from various disciplines, including psychology, neuroscience, and body-centered practices such as yoga and mindfulness. By understanding the theoretical underpinnings of somatic psychotherapy, practitioners can effectively utilize body-oriented techniques to promote self-awareness, emotional regulation, and holistic healing.

2.1 Body-Mind Connection in Trauma

The interaction and reciprocal effect of bodily sensations, emotions, and traumatic events are referred to as the "body-mind connection" in trauma. The effects of a traumatic incident go beyond only psychological suffering; they can cause disruptions in the body's natural functions. Physical signs and feelings are another way that trauma may appear.

The body's reaction mechanism, which includes the autonomic nervous system, activates in a fight-flight-freeze response when a traumatic incident occurs. These physiological responses set up the body to either face the danger or run away from it. The energy produced by the body's reaction, however, might become trapped or blocked under circumstances where the danger cannot be successfully faced or evacuated, with long-lasting physical and psychological repercussions.

The effects of trauma on the body may take many different forms. Physical symptoms include persistent discomfort, tense muscles, digestive problems, headaches, and changes in sleep habits. Trauma may cause anxiety, sadness, mood fluctuations, hyperarousal, or emotional numbness on an emotional level. Additionally, cognitive functions including memory, focus, and decision-making may be impacted by trauma.

Trauma is recognized as a physical experience as well as a cerebral and emotional one by somatic psychotherapy. Somatic methods to trauma seek to accelerate recovery by easing the release and integration of the energy and sensations that have been imprisoned by the traumatic experience. People may re-establish a connection with their bodies, control their physiological reactions, and increase their resilience by being aware of their physical sensations and partaking in body-focused activities like breathwork, movement, and body awareness exercises.

The body has the key to unlocking and digesting traumatic events, according to somatic psychotherapy. People may access and process their trauma memories, let go of tension and energy that has been holding them back, and gradually regain their feeling of security and well-being via the body-mind connection. Somatic psychotherapy may provide a thorough and complete approach to recovery by addressing the physical components of trauma, encouraging integration and harmony between the body and mind.

2.2 Key Theories and Models in Somatic Psychotherapy

In psychotherapy, a number of fundamental ideas and models have been created expressly for the treatment of trauma. These methodologies provide concepts and tactics for comprehending and dealing with the effects of trauma on people. Several of the well-known hypotheses and models are listed below:

1. Cognitive behavioral therapy with a focus on trauma (TF-CBT): To treat the cognitive, emotional, and behavioral impacts of trauma, TF-CBT integrates cognitive and behavioral approaches. It emphasizes on assisting people in processing traumatic experiences, learning coping mechanisms, and refuting irrational assumptions about the trauma.

2. Internal Family Systems (IFS): The IFS model is centered on comprehending and interacting with the many components or features of a person's internal system. In order to encourage healing and integration, it aids people in recognizing their many parts, including those that store painful experiences, and developing a caring connection with them.

3. Narrative therapy: Narrative therapy helps people rebuild their personal narratives in a manner that promotes resilience and empowerment by examining the meaning people assign to their traumatic experiences. It tries to liberate people from the prevailing trauma narrative while allowing them to rewrite and reinterpret their own tales.

4. Models based on attachment: Attachment theory is used into many attachment-based treatments, including Attachment-Focused EMDR and Emotionally Focused Therapy (EFT), which highlight the significance of developing safe and secure connections to facilitate trauma recovery.

These theories and models provide a variety of trauma treatment modalities, each with a special focus and set of methods. Depending on the client's requirements and preferences, psychotherapists may modify and include a variety of treatments, with the ultimate goal of fostering healing, posttraumatic development, and the restoration of well-being.

2.2.1 Somatic Experiencing

Dr. Peter A. Levine created the therapy technique known as somatic Experiencing (SE), which aims to heal trauma and its repercussions on the neurological system. It is predicated on the knowledge that traumatic experiences might impair the body's innate ability to recover and self-regulate.

The autonomic nerve system (ANS), the area of our neural system in charge of regulating automatic physiological activities, is said by SE to be dysregulated after trauma. The ANS may become trapped in a state of fight, flight, or freeze when confronted with overwhelming circumstances, resulting in a variety of physical and psychological symptoms.

Somatic experience aims to assist people in progressively and securely gaining access to and releasing the energy and feelings connected with traumatic situations. This is accomplished using a technique known as titration, which entails tackling digestible chunks of the trauma rather than overwhelming the person.

In SE, the therapist assists the patient in keeping track of their physical sensations, paying attention to them, and observing any uncontrollable movements or urges. People may start to regain their natural capacity to self-regulate and heal by bringing attention to these bodily sensations in a secure and encouraging atmosphere.

The necessity of pendulation, which entails switching between traumatic activation (fight-or-flight), and the body's natural resources (resourcing), such as emotions of security, tranquillity, and support, is another point stressed by SE. Individuals may progressively develop a tolerance for the activation brought on by trauma by alternating between these states while also integrating fresh perceptions of safety and controlled arousal.

It's crucial to remember that somatic experience is a compassionate, client-centered method that honors each person's specific processing speed and capacity for trauma. Individuals are not required to recount or relive the horrific experience in detail. Instead, emphasis is placed on fostering a feeling of safety, reestablishing physiological equilibrium, and enabling the body's own healing mechanisms to take place.

Somatic experience has been shown to be useful in easing the effects of trauma, boosting self-control, and boosting general wellbeing. It may be used to treat a variety of traumatic events, such as one-time traumas, childhood traumas, and ongoing pressures.

Before applying this strategy in therapeutic settings, practitioners should be properly trained and experienced since somatic experiencing certification involves specific training and supervision. People may traverse their journeys of healing and recovery from trauma in a safe and supportive setting under the direction of a qualified somatic experience therapist.

2.2.2 Sensorimotor Psychotherapy

The link between the body and mind in the processing of trauma and other psychological disorders is the subject of Sensory Motor Psychotherapy (SMP), a body-oriented therapeutic method. Pat Ogden, a psychologist and innovator in the area of somatic psychology, created it.

SMP takes into account the effects of trauma on the body and works to encourage recovery by integrating ideas from attachment theory, neuroscience, and body-centered methods. It acknowledges that traumatic events are preserved in the body's sensory and motor patterns in addition to memories and emotions.

The goal of the treatment is to assist patients in becoming more conscious of their physical feelings, movements, and postures so they may access and deal with unresolved trauma. SMP aims to enhance integration between ideas, emotions, and physical sensations while restoring autonomic nervous system homeostasis via the gentle and thoughtful exploration of body experiences.

The emphasis on the "here and now" experience is one of the main components of SMP. SMP encourages clients to observe and pay attention to their present-moment body feelings and movements rather than focusing primarily on understanding or talking about traumatic situations. Exercises like breathwork, moderate movement, guided visualization, and heightened bodily awareness may all be used for this.

The use of attachment theory ideas is a key component of SMP. The therapist assists the patient in recognizing and examining the ways that their patterns of self- and other-relationship may have been influenced by early attachment experiences. SMP strives to assist the development of secure relationships by focusing on interpersonal dynamics and the body's felt sense.

Other somatic therapies that may be used during sensory motor psychotherapy include somatic contact, replenishing exercises, and grounding procedures. These methods may aid people in calming their nerve systems, releasing tension from their muscles, and developing a feeling of security and embodiment.

SMP promotes the integration of fragmented or disowned components of self and aids the processing and resolution of traumatic memories and emotions by addressing the body-mind link. It may support people in gaining more self-awareness, resilience, and a rounded, embodied sense of self.

It is essential to stress that practitioners of Sensory Motor Psychotherapy need particular training and oversight. By addressing the somatic, sensory, and motor components of their experiences, people may take a holistic and all-encompassing approach to healing trauma and improving wellbeing under the direction of a qualified SMP therapist.

2.2.3 Bodynamic Psychotherapy

Bodynamic Psychotherapy is a body-centered kind of treatment that emphasizes the fusion of a person's psychological, emotional, and physical selves. It blends knowledge from the fields of psychology, neuroscience, and body-centered practices to comprehend and use the body as an essential tool for healing and personal development.

Bodynamic Psychotherapy, created by Lisbeth Marcher and other industry pioneers, lays a focus on understanding character structures and the influence of early events on a person's development. It acknowledges the close connection between physical holding patterns in the body and patterns of behavior, relationships, and emotional reactions.

The evaluation of the client's character structure, which entails locating muscle tension patterns and postural responses connected to certain psychological and emotional difficulties, is the first step in the therapeutic process. Bodynamic Psychotherapy seeks to relieve muscle tension and expedite the healing of underlying psychological issues by bringing awareness to these physiological patterns.

Bodynamic Psychotherapy employs a variety of body-oriented approaches and treatments throughout the therapeutic process to meet the unique requirements of each patient. The exploration and integration of emotional, cognitive, and bodily experiences may be supported by hands-on work, gentle movements, breathwork, and vocal dialogues.

The fundamental tenets of bodynamic psychotherapy are founded on the conviction that each person has inborn abilities and skills for healing and development. Clients may access and integrate their experiences, let go of painful imprints, and create more adaptable relationships with both themselves and others by working with the body and its knowledge.

Increasing self-awareness, supporting emotional control, enhancing interpersonal connections, and building a feeling of embodiment and vitality are some of the therapeutic objectives of bodynamic psychotherapy. In order to help clients manage the obstacles of life with more resilience and satisfaction, it strives to assist their development of a more true and balanced sense of self.

The practice of bodynamic psychotherapy requires particular education and experience, it should be noted. With a thorough and integrated approach to resolving psychological issues and fostering personal development, therapists educated in this technique are adept at dealing with both verbal and non-verbal parts of the therapeutic process.

2.2.4 Hakomi Method

In order to assist profound human development and healing, the Hakomi Method is a psychotherapy technique that combines concepts from mindfulness, somatics (body-oriented practices), and psychodynamic psychology. Hakomi, which Ron Kurtz created, has roots in both Western psychology and Eastern philosophical traditions.

The Hakomi Method's guiding principles are based on mindfulness, nonviolence, oneness, and organicity. An individual's view of themselves and the world is shaped by their unconscious belief systems, basic memories, and creative patterns, which the treatment tries to investigate and modify.

The use of mindfulness, which entails bringing non-judgmental awareness to present-moment events, is one of the fundamental components of Hakomi. People who practice mindfulness may develop understanding of the underlying ideas, feelings, and bodily sensations that underlie their actions, interactions, and relationships.

The body's knowledge should be used in treatment, according to Hakomi. The therapist assists clients in accessing and integrating somatic experiences that may provide insightful information and promote emotional healing via gentle and non-intrusive touch, body awareness exercises, and movement exploration.

Hakomi therapy is client-centered and collaborative, with the therapist paying close attention to each client's unique requirements and pace. The therapist creates a loving and comfortable atmosphere that encourages trust and aids the client in discovering their inner selves.

Hakomi uses a range of methods to assist clients in identifying and comprehending their unconscious patterns and belief systems, including guided imagery, role-playing, and somatic experimentation. Clients are encouraged to explore their fundamental thoughts and feelings, have an internal conversation, and reframe and modify their experiences using these strategies.

The Hakomi Method acknowledges the significance of early experiences and how they affect how someone develops their ideas and behaviors. Clients may better understand themselves and the causes of their problems by examining their fundamental memories and the manner in which they have shaped their present-day experiences.

Supporting people on their path of self-discovery, healing, and progress is the ultimate purpose of hakomi therapy. Hakomi is a multifaceted therapeutic method that addresses the mind, body, and spirit by fusing mindfulness, somatic awareness, and psychological investigation.

The Hakomi Method's practitioners go through lengthy training in order to get the knowledge and compassion needed to support clients through this transforming process. Hakomi offers clients the chance to receive significant insights, grow in self-compassion, and bring about long-lasting change in their life since it is a profoundly experiential technique.

2.2.5 EMDR (Eye Movement Desensitization and Reprocessing)

Dr. Francine Shapiro created the therapy method known as Eye Movement Desensitization and Reprocessing (EMDR), which aims to cure traumatic memories and other upsetting situations. It is predicated on the knowledge that traumatic memories may persist and obstruct the brain's typical information processing function.

An organized eight-phase therapy process is used in EMDR. The therapist leads the client through bilateral stimulation throughout this procedure, which may be done via eye movements, noises, or tactile sensations. The brain's natural information processing machinery is activated by the bilateral stimulation, which aids in the reprocessing of traumatic memories.

Establishing a secure and reliable therapeutic connection is the first step in therapy. The next step is for the client and the therapist to decide which particular traumatic memory or target will serve as the main focus of the EMDR session. The client is asked to recall the memories along with any accompanying unfavorable thoughts, feelings, or bodily sensations.

The therapist leads the client in bilateral stimulation while the memory is being kept in mind, such as having them follow the therapist's fingers with their eyes. The client is asked to allow their thoughts wander and take note of any fresh ideas, feelings, or physical sensations that come to mind while the bilateral stimulation takes place. This technique keeps on until the anguish brought on by the memory has greatly decreased or vanished.

Positive belief or cognitive installation is another EMDR component. After the anguish brought on by the traumatic memory has subsided, the therapist helps the client find and incorporate empowering beliefs that balance out the unfavorable ones brought on by the traumatic event.

The therapist occasionally checks in with the patient over the course of the therapy to assure their general wellbeing and to evaluate the progress achieved in reprocessing the traumatic memory. EMDR may be used to treat both simple traumas and complicated traumas, as well as other unpleasant situations. Simple traumas include attacks and vehicle accidents.

The symptoms of PTSD (Post-Traumatic Stress Disorder), anxiety, sadness, and other trauma-related issues may be effectively treated using EMDR, according to research. Bilateral stimulation, a key component of EMDR, is thought to aid in accessing and reprocessing traumatic memories that have been stored in an adaptive manner, enabling the integration of the event into a deeper awareness of the self.

Specialized instruction and oversight are required for EMDR certification. By adhering to the established procedures and recommendations for the use of this therapeutic method, skilled and licensed mental health practitioners should provide EMDR treatment.

The Role of the Nervous System in Trauma

The experience and reaction to trauma are greatly influenced by the neurological system. Trauma is defined as a traumatic occurrence or experience that is too upsetting or overwhelming for a person to handle. As part of the body's natural survival reaction, the nervous system is quickly triggered when a traumatic event takes place.

The nervous system is in charge of absorbing environmental information, processing it, and organizing the proper reactions. The fight-or-flight response, which is mediated by the autonomic nervous system, is a state of heightened alertness that the body enters when trauma takes place. This reaction gets the body ready to face or run from the imagined danger.

The sympathetic branch of the autonomic nervous system is engaged in the immediate aftermath of trauma, increasing heart rate, blood pressure, and breathing as well as causing the production of stress chemicals including cortisol and adrenaline. This physiological reaction is intended to aid the body in responding to the danger in a powerful way.

The nervous system is involved in the fight-or-flight response as well as the emotional and cognitive reactions to trauma. The amygdala, one of the brain's emotional regions, is heavily engaged in the production and control of the emotions connected to trauma, such as fear, anxiety, and hypervigilance. The brain analyzes and interprets the traumatic event.

The way the nervous system reacts to trauma may affect a person's health in both the short- and long-term. The nervous system's activity may aid people in surviving and overcoming an urgent danger in the short term. It may, however, overwhelm the nervous system's ability to control arousal and emotions if the trauma is severe or protracted, which can result in symptoms of trauma-related diseases including post-traumatic stress disorder (PTSD).

Symptoms of PTSD include persistent and upsetting memories or thoughts of the event, avoiding triggers associated with it, changes in mood and cognition, and increased arousal. The functioning of the neurological system, including changes in neurotransmitter levels, neuronal circuitry, and the stress response, is considered to be affected by these symptoms.

Other physiological systems in the body may be impacted by the neurological system's reaction to stress. Chronic stress response activation has been linked to the emergence of physical health difficulties such immune system malfunction, gastrointestinal disorders, and cardiovascular disease.

It is crucial to comprehend how the neurological system is affected by trauma in order to create effective interventions and therapies for illnesses associated to trauma. Eye movement desensitization and reprocessing (EMDR), a treatment that targets the nervous system, aims to control the nervous system's reaction to stress while assisting people in processing and integrating their traumatic experiences.

In general, the nervous system is crucial to how trauma is experienced and handled. It facilitates the body's rapid physiological reaction to the danger and aids in the trauma's emotional and mental healing. Promoting healing and recovery from trauma-related diseases requires recognizing and treating the effects of trauma on the neurological system.

3.1 Understanding the Autonomic Nervous System

The body's reaction to trauma is significantly influenced by the autonomic nervous system (ANS). It is a part of the peripheral nervous system that regulates a variety of physiological processes alongside the central nervous system (CNS), including many of the body's involuntary activities.

The ANS is engaged by a traumatic incident and affects the body's initial reaction by preparing it to either face or flee from the perceived danger. The sympathetic nervous system (SNS) and the parasympathetic nervous system (PNS) are the two primary parts of this reaction, which is also known as the fight-or-flight response.

1. Sympathetic Nervous System (SNS): In response to a danger, the SNS is in charge of releasing stored energy and boosting the body's ability to exert itself physically. It causes a number of physiological changes, such as:
- Elevated heart rate and blood pressure: The SNS tells the heart to beat more quickly and forcefully, delivering more blood and oxygen to the muscles and other critical organs.
- Dilate pupils: The SNS expands the pupils to improve visual acuity and make it possible to notice potential dangers more effectively.
- Increased respiration rate: The SNS speeds up breathing to enhance oxygen absorption and provide the body more energy for exercise.
- Adrenal gland activation: The SNS triggers the adrenal glands to produce stress chemicals including adrenaline (epinephrine) and noradrenaline (norepinephrine). By

enhancing the body's physiological reaction to stress, these hormones also raise attentiveness and general preparedness for action.
- Suppression of non-essential body activities: To save energy and allocate resources toward immediate survival, the SNS limits non-essential biological functions including digestion and reproduction.

2. Parasympathetic Nervous System (PNS): After the danger has gone, the PNS works as a counterweight to the SNS, assisting in bringing the body back into harmony and calm. Rest, relaxation, and the restoration of body functioning are encouraged. The PNS performs a number of crucial duties, including
- Slowing heart rate: In order to get the heart rate back to normal resting levels, the PNS slows it down.
- Pupils are constricted by the PNS in order to preserve energy and decrease visual sensitivity.
- Stimulating digestion: The PNS promotes the generation of digestive enzymes and boosts blood flow to the digestive organs, hence activating digestion.

Trauma-related dysregulation of the ANS's response might make it challenging to recover from the traumatic experience. Trauma-related diseases, such post-traumatic stress disorder (PTSD), are often characterized by an overactive SNS and a decreased capacity to activate the PNS, which leads to persistent physiological arousal and emotional dysregulation in those who have these disorders.

Trauma-related ANS dysregulation may have a number of effects. Chronic SNS activation may cause symptoms including hypervigilance, heightened startle reactions, and trouble falling asleep. Chronic stress hormone release may also impair physical health by suppressing the immune system, causing more inflammation, and causing cardiovascular issues.

The goal of ANS-focused treatments for trauma is to balance and regulate the autonomic response. Deep breathing exercises, mindfulness exercises, and relaxation methods may all help to activate the PNS and foster a feeling of peace and relaxation. The goal of trauma-focused treatments like eye movement desensitization and reprocessing (EMDR), which helps to control the ANS and lessen symptoms associated with trauma, is to reprocess painful memories and desensitize the body's reaction to trauma triggers.

Effective treatment and recovery from trauma-related diseases, as well as the promotion of healing and the restoration of balance to the body's physiological response, depend on an understanding of and attention to the function of the autonomic nervous system in trauma.

3.2 Polyvagal Theory and Trauma Responses

Dr. Stephen Porges' polyvagal theory provides a framework for comprehending how the autonomic nervous system (ANS) reacts to stress and trauma. The Social Engagement System, the Fight-or-Flight reaction, and the Freeze response are suggested to be the three different response states of the ANS.

According to the hypothesis, the physiological condition linked to emotions of security and connection is the Social Engagement System. It involves the ventral vagal complex, which encourages social interaction and connection with others, being activated. The Social Engagement System encourages beneficial interactions and stress-adaptive reactions when a person feels secure and supported.

However, the ANS may trigger the Fight-or-Flight response when a danger is recognized. The sympathetic branch of the ANS is responsible for this reaction, which results in an increase in heart rate, respiration, and energy mobilization. The fight-or-flight reaction gets someone ready to take action, either to defend themselves from the danger or to run away from it.

The Freeze reaction may happen if the Fight-or-Flight response fails to successfully counter the perceived danger or if the threat is too great. The dorsal vagal complex is involved in this reaction, which causes immobility, dissociation, and a shutdown of body activities. As a means of coping with the overwhelming traumatic event, people may feel numb, disconnected, and dissociated in this condition.

Depending on the person and the particular traumatic incident, trauma reactions might differ. Some people may primarily display fight-or-flight behaviors, which include being on high alert, easily startled, and prone to rage or aggressiveness. Others could primarily display Freeze reactions, which include dissociation, a sense of disconnection from their body, or trouble recalling the event.

Understanding how trauma reactions are founded in the autonomic nervous system's efforts to control and adapt to perceived dangers is made possible by the polyvagal hypothesis. Given that the Social interaction System is so important for healing and rehabilitation, it emphasizes the need of fostering safety and encouraging social interaction for those who have suffered trauma. Therapists and other healthcare providers may design treatments to best help people in controlling their autonomic reactions and recovering from trauma by knowing these various response states. Dr. Stephen Porges' Polyvagal theory offers a thorough explanation of how the autonomic nervous system (ANS) reacts to stress and trauma. The fight-or-flight reaction, the social engagement system, and the freeze response are described as three separate response patterns.

1. Social Engagement System: This reaction is related to emotions of social connection, safety, and trust. The ventral vagal complex, which controls social interaction and communication activities, is involved in this process. People feel at ease, calm, and capable of engaging with people in a

healthy and adaptive manner when the social engagement system is active.

2. Fight-or-Flight Response: This reaction occurs when a danger is detected and the sympathetic branch of the ANS is activated. The body is prepared for fighting or escaping from the danger as a result of increased heart rate, blood pressure, and adrenaline release. In circumstances when immediate action is necessary to guarantee survival, this reaction is adaptive.

3. Freeze reaction: The dorsal vagal complex, which is connected to immobility, dissociation, and a shutdown of body activities, mediates the freeze reaction. When the fight-or-flight response fails to adequately meet the perceived danger or when the threat is too great, this reaction takes place. It is an adaptive tactic to defend oneself when fleeing or engaging in combat is not an option.

Depending on the condition of their ANS, people may display various trauma reactions while experiencing trauma. Some people may predominantly exhibit fight-or-flight reactions, which are marked by anxiety, hypervigilance, and an impulsive or hostile response to perceived dangers. Some people may primarily exhibit freeze reactions, which are marked by disconnection, numbness, and a feeling of helplessness or hopelessness.

The polyvagal hypothesis emphasizes the value of the social engagement system in the healing process after trauma. The activation of the ventral vagal complex and the encouragement of a healing response depend on the development of a feeling of safety, trust, and social connection. Individuals may control their ANS reactions and recover from trauma with the use of therapeutic approaches that emphasize resilience development, enhanced social support, and co-regulation.

Healthcare workers may create trauma-informed strategies that meet people's unique reaction patterns by understanding the polyvagal hypothesis. Interventions that are specifically designed to stimulate the social engagement system, lessen hypervigilance or detachment, and promote a feeling of safety may aid trauma recovery and assist people in regaining autonomic nervous system equilibrium.

3.3 Window of Tolerance and Regulation

The ability of a person to successfully manage and control their emotions and arousal levels is known as the "window of tolerance." A person may feel reasonably stable and be at their best while they are in a variety of emotional and physiological states.

People who have experienced trauma may have trouble controlling their emotions and degree of arousal. Trauma may alter a person's window of tolerance, making them more susceptible to feeling overwhelmed, dysregulated, and helpless in the face of stresses. Hypervigilance, anxiety, flashbacks, dissociation, and emotional reactivity are a few symptoms that may result from this.

When emotions or arousal levels become unbalanced, regulation refers to the capacity to put oneself back within the window of tolerance. It encompasses techniques and abilities that support people in self-soothing, calming their nervous systems, and regaining a feeling of security and equilibrium.

The goal of therapeutic therapies that emphasize regulation in trauma is to assist people in enlarging and strengthening their window of tolerance. To control emotions and arousal levels, practitioners might use methods including deep breathing, mindfulness, grounding exercises, sensory self-soothing, and progressive muscle relaxation. It's also essential to the regulation process to establish a feeling of security, trust, and connection with a reliable therapist or support network.

In order to operate more successfully and participate in the healing process of trauma, people may learn how to manage their emotional experiences and endure suffering without getting overwhelmed by it by developing their regulating abilities.

Assessing and Evaluating Trauma

Understanding the effects of traumatic events on a person's mental, emotional, and physical health requires first assessing and analyzing trauma. Trauma evaluations seek to compile detailed data on the kind of trauma, the person's present symptoms and functioning, and the best course of therapy.

Typically, a mix of interviews, self-report questionnaires, and clinical observations are used to assess trauma. The nature and degree of the traumatic events the person encountered, their mental and physical responses, as well as any accompanying symptoms and impairments, will all be gathered by the clinicians.

Assessing for trauma-related illnesses like post-traumatic stress disorder (PTSD) or other trauma-related ailments may be part of the evaluation of trauma. Assessing for symptoms like hyperarousal, avoidance behavior, intrusive thoughts or recollections, and changes in mood or cognition may be part of this.

The evaluation method takes into account a number of variables that may affect a person's reaction to trauma, including pre-existing mental health issues, social support networks, cultural background, and other contextual variables. To obtain a thorough knowledge of the individual's experiences, trauma evaluation must be approached holistically and with cultural sensitivity.

The main objective of a trauma assessment and evaluation is to accurately identify the trauma history, present symptoms, and functional limitations of the person. This knowledge directs the creation of a personalized treatment plan and aids therapists and medical personnel in offering the proper treatments and support needed for trauma recovery.

4.1 Trauma Assessment Tools and Interviews

To assist in the thorough assessment of traumatic events and associated symptoms, a number of trauma assessment methods and interviews have been created. These evaluation tools were created with the express purpose of learning more about the kind and effect of trauma on a person's psychological, emotional, and physical health. Typical trauma evaluation instruments and interview questions include:

PTSD Scale for DSM-5 (Clinician-Administered): According to the DSM-5 criteria, this structured interview is often used to evaluate and diagnose post-traumatic stress disorder (PTSD). It looks at if trauma-related symptoms including reliving, avoiding, having bad mood and cognition swings, and hyperarousal are present and how severe they are.

2. TSI-2 (Traumatic Symptom Inventory-2): A self-report questionnaire called the TSI-2 evaluates a variety of trauma-related symptoms and challenges. Dissociation, anxiety, sadness, rage, sexual issues, sleep issues, and physical symptoms are just a few of the topics it tackles.

3. The Impact of incident Scale-Revised (IES-R) measures the intensity of intrusive thoughts, avoidance, and hyperarousal symptoms linked to a particular traumatic incident. It is often used to determine how acute trauma has affected a person and is especially useful when determining how recent traumatic events have affected a person's symptoms.

4. The Dissociative Experiences Scale (DES) measures the frequency and severity of dissociative experiences that may develop in response to trauma. The DES aids in determining if dissociation is present and how severe it is since it is a prevalent coping strategy in trauma.

5. Structured Clinical Interview for Disorders According to the DSM-5 (SCID): The SCID is a commonly used diagnostic tool for screening many mental illnesses, including PTSD and other trauma-related problems, even though it is not trauma-specific. It offers a thorough and organized interview process that addresses every need for a precise diagnosis.

The utilization of clinical interviews and open-ended inquiries by therapists in addition to these standardized assessment methods may help them learn more about a patient's trauma history, effects, and subjective experiences. People get the chance to share their stories during these interviews, giving the evaluation process context.

While these assessment tools are helpful, it's crucial to remember that they should be used in combination with a thorough clinical examination. In interpreting the findings and appreciating each person's particular experiences, the therapist or assessor's skill and sensibility are crucial. Additionally, it's important to do trauma evaluations in a setting that is secure and encouraging while maintaining anonymity and providing the right kind of aftercare.

4.2 Identifying Somatic Symptoms and Signs of Trauma

Somatic symptoms refer to physical sensations or experiences that are associated with trauma. Traumatic experiences can have a significant impact on the body, leading to various somatic symptoms and signs. It is important to note that somatic symptoms can vary widely among individuals, and not everyone will experience the same physical manifestations of trauma. However, some common somatic symptoms and signs of trauma include:

1. Body tension and pain: Individuals who have experienced trauma may frequently experience muscle tension, stiffness, or pain, particularly in areas such as the neck, shoulders, and back. This tension and pain can be a result of the body's physiological response to stress and the chronic activation of the fight-or-flight response.

2. Gastrointestinal issues: Trauma can affect the digestive system and lead to gastrointestinal symptoms such as stomachaches, irritable bowel syndrome (IBS), nausea, or diarrhea. These symptoms can arise due to the dysregulation of the autonomic nervous system and disturbances in the gut-brain axis.

3. Hypervigilance and sensory sensitivity: Trauma survivors may be hyperalert and have heightened sensory sensitivity. They may struggle with coping with sensory input, such as loud noises, bright lights, or crowded places, as these can trigger feelings of overwhelm and anxiety.

4. Sleep disturbances: Trauma can disrupt sleep patterns and lead to difficulties falling asleep, staying asleep, or experiencing restful sleep. Individuals may have vivid nightmares or experience night sweats, leading to chronic fatigue and low energy levels.

5. Physical health problems: Trauma can increase the risk of developing physical health conditions, including cardiovascular issues, chronic pain conditions, autoimmune disorders, and immune system dysregulation. The chronic activation of stress responses can impact the body's overall functioning and contribute to the development of these health problems.

6. Changes in appetite and eating patterns: Trauma survivors may experience changes in appetite, leading to either increased or decreased food intake. Some individuals may use food as a way to cope with emotional distress, leading to disordered eating patterns or weight fluctuations.

7. Sensations of numbness and disconnection: Trauma can result in feelings of numbness or disconnection from the body, making it challenging for individuals to experience physical sensations or emotions. This dissociative response is the body's way of protecting itself from overwhelming experiences.

8. Chronic headaches or migraines: Trauma can contribute to the development of chronic headaches or migraines. These headaches may be tension-related or result from high levels of stress and anxiety.

4.3 Establishing Safety and Trust in the Therapeutic Relationship

In order to establish safety and trust in therapeutic relationships, several key elements should be considered:

1. Confidentiality: Ensuring that client information is held in strict confidence is crucial in fostering trust. Therapists must adhere to ethical guidelines and legal obligations regarding client privacy and confidentiality.

2. Active listening: Active listening involves fully engaging with the client and giving them your full attention. It is important for therapists to demonstrate empathy, validate client experiences, and show genuine interest in their concerns.

3. Establishing clear boundaries: Setting clear boundaries with clients helps establish a professional and safe therapeutic relationship. This includes discussing the limits of confidentiality, appropriate modes of communication, and the therapist's availability.

4. Building rapport: Building rapport is key to establishing trust. Therapists should create a warm and non-judgmental atmosphere where clients feel comfortable sharing their feelings and experiences.

5. Collaborative decision-making: Inviting clients to actively participate in their therapy sessions and treatment planning helps build trust. Clients should be informed about their

treatment options and have their preferences and goals taken into account.

6. Consistency and reliability: Being consistent and reliable in attending scheduled sessions and adhering to agreed-upon treatment plans helps build trust. It demonstrates the therapist's commitment to the therapeutic process and client well-being.

7. Transparency and honesty: Therapists should be transparent and honest with clients about their qualifications, experience, and any potential limitations. This helps create a foundation of trust and ensures that clients feel informed and empowered in their therapy journey.

8. Cultural sensitivity and respect: Therapists should strive to be culturally sensitive and respectful, recognizing and valuing diversity. This includes being aware of cultural differences and how they may impact the therapeutic relationship.

9. Addressing power imbalances: Therapists hold a position of power in the therapeutic relationship, and it's important to be mindful of this dynamic and actively work to reduce power imbalances. This can be done through open communication, empowering clients, and seeking collaborative decision-making.

10. Regular feedback and evaluation: Seeking regular feedback from clients about their experiences in therapy can contribute to building trust and improving the therapeutic relationship. This feedback can be used to address any

concerns, make adjustments to the treatment plan if needed, and ensure that clients feel heard and valued.

By consistently applying these principles, therapists can establish safety and trust in therapeutic relationships, creating a supportive and empowering environment for clients to explore their concerns and work towards positive change.

Somatic Techniques and Interventions

Somatic techniques and interventions focus on the mind-body connection and the experience of the body in therapeutic work. They recognize that our bodies hold valuable information and can be powerful allies in the healing process. Somatic techniques involve bringing attention to bodily sensations, movement, and breath to increase self-awareness and promote healing.

By engaging with the body, individuals can gain insight into their emotions, beliefs, and patterns, and work towards resolving past traumas and restoring balance. Somatic interventions can include practices such as body-centered mindfulness, biofeedback, somatic experiencing, and yoga therapy. These approaches can be effective in addressing a variety of psychological, emotional, and physical challenges, and can complement traditional talk therapy approaches.

5.1 Grounding and Centering Practices

Grounding and centering practices are techniques that help individuals regulate their body and mind in the present moment, promoting feelings of safety and stability. These practices are particularly beneficial for individuals who have experienced trauma.

Traumatic experiences can often leave individuals feeling disconnected from their bodies and overwhelmed by intense emotions and sensations. Grounding techniques help individuals reconnect with their physical bodies and the present moment, providing a sense of stability and safety.

Some common grounding practices include:

1. Deep breathing: Taking slow, deep breaths can help regulate the nervous system and promote a sense of calmness.

2. Sensory focus: Directing attention to the senses by noticing specific sensations, such as the feeling of the feet on the ground, the touch of an object, or the smells in the environment.

3. Visualization: Imagining a safe and peaceful place or picturing a grounding object can help individuals create a sense of stability and safety.

4. Body scanning: Paying attention to different parts of the body and noticing any sensations or tension can increase body awareness and grounding.

Centering practices, on the other hand, involve finding a point of balance within oneself. This may include focusing on one's breath, connecting to a core sense of self, or engaging in mindfulness practices. Centering can help individuals maintain emotional balance and make decisions from a place of inner wisdom and clarity.

When trauma occurs, individuals often feel a loss of control and a disconnection from their sense of self. Centering practices provide a way to reconnect with one's inner resources and regain a sense of personal power and agency.

In the context of trauma, grounding and centering practices can support individuals in managing overwhelming emotions, reducing anxiety and hypervigilance, and promoting a sense of safety and control. These practices help individuals feel more present and anchored in the here and now, rather than being overwhelmed by traumatic memories or triggers.

It's important to note that different grounding and centering techniques work better for different individuals, and it may take some exploration to find the practices that resonate the most. Therapists, trauma-informed yoga instructors, and other professionals trained in trauma work can provide guidance and support in using these techniques effectively in the healing journey.

5.2 Breathwork and Body Awareness

Breathwork and body awareness are powerful tools that can be used in trauma healing and recovery. They can help individuals regulate their nervous system, release stored trauma, and cultivate a greater sense of safety and ease within their bodies.

Breathwork involves intentionally focusing on and manipulating the breath to promote relaxation, stress reduction, and emotional regulation. Different types of breathwork techniques, such as deep belly breathing, diaphragmatic breathing, or alternate nostril breathing, can be used to activate the parasympathetic nervous system and induce a state of calmness.

When it comes to trauma, the breath is intimately connected to the body's stress response. Traumatic experiences often result in a dysregulated nervous system, leading to hypervigilance, anxiety, and emotional instability. By engaging in breathwork practices, individuals can learn to regulate their breath and activate the body's relaxation response, helping to downregulate the stress response and reduce emotional distress.

Body awareness refers to the practice of tuning into and paying attention to the sensations, feelings, and movements of the body. Trauma often disrupts the mind-body connection and can leave individuals feeling disconnected or dissociated from their physical selves.

By intentionally focusing on body sensations, individuals can anchor themselves in the present moment and cultivate a greater sense of safety in their bodies. Body awareness techniques can include practices such as body scans, progressive muscle relaxation, or gentle movement exercises like yoga or tai chi.

For individuals who have experienced trauma, body awareness can help dissolve the tension and holding patterns that may have become ingrained in the body as a result of the traumatic experience. It can also facilitate the release and processing of trapped emotions or traumatic memories stored in the body.

By combining breathwork and body awareness, individuals can develop a greater sense of agency and control over their physical and emotional experiences. These practices can support individuals in finding a greater sense of safety, grounding, and self-regulation, which are important aspects of the healing journey from trauma.

5.3 Somatic Tracking and Felt Sense

Somatic tracking and felt sense are somatic practices that can be beneficial in trauma healing and recovery. They involve tuning into the body's sensations and accessing the wisdom and information that arises from within.

Somatic tracking involves consciously and attentively following bodily sensations and experiences as they arise in the present moment. It is a practice of observing and tracking the various sensations and movements that occur in the body, without judgment or trying to change anything. This practice helps individuals become more aware of their bodily experiences, allowing them to notice subtle shifts, tensions, or other sensations that may be related to traumatic experiences.

Felt sense refers to the bodily-felt experiences and sensations that arise in response to a specific situation, memory, or emotion. It involves attending to the subtle nuances and intricacies of bodily sensations that go beyond simply identifying basic physical sensations. The felt sense provides a more holistic understanding of the body's response to an event or circumstance and can offer valuable insights into the underlying emotions, beliefs, and patterns associated with trauma.

In the context of trauma, somatic tracking and felt sense practices help individuals develop a deeper connection with their bodies, as well as a more profound understanding of how trauma is held and experienced in the body. By tracking sensations and exploring the felt sense, individuals can gradually uncover and process unresolved trauma, release tension and holding patterns, and gain insights into the relational and emotional dynamics connected to their traumatic experiences.

Somatic tracking and felt sense practices are often used in conjunction with other therapeutic modalities, such as somatic experiencing, Sensorimotor Psychotherapy, or trauma-informed yoga. These approaches recognize that trauma is stored in the body and that healing involves addressing both the physical and psychological aspects of trauma.

It's important to note that somatic tracking and working with the felt sense should be done with the guidance of a trained professional, particularly for individuals who have experienced trauma. Trauma-informed therapists and somatic practitioners can provide the necessary support and create a safe container for individuals to explore their bodily experiences in a regulated and contained manner. They can help individuals navigate any intensity or discomfort that may arise during the process and provide strategies for grounding and self-regulation as needed.

5.4 Body-oriented Interventions (e.g., Movement, Yoga, Tai Chi)

Body-oriented interventions such as movement practices, yoga, and tai chi have shown promise in supporting the healing of trauma. These interventions recognize the interconnectedness of the mind and body and use movement, breath, and mindfulness to promote healing and integration.

Movement practices, such as dance or expressive movement, can help individuals release tension and pent-up emotions stored in the body. Movement allows for the expression of feelings that may be otherwise difficult to access or communicate verbally. These practices can promote a sense of freedom, empowerment, and embodiment, supporting individuals in reconnecting with their bodies and reclaiming their physical agency.

Yoga is a holistic practice that combines physical postures, breathwork, and meditation. Trauma-sensitive or trauma-informed yoga approaches adapt yoga practices to create a safe and supportive environment for individuals with trauma histories. These approaches emphasize choice, agency, and self-regulation, encouraging participants to listen to their bodies and make decisions based on their current needs and comfort.

Yoga helps individuals build body awareness, regulate their nervous systems, and cultivate a sense of grounding and stability. Certain yoga poses and breathing techniques can be particularly beneficial for trauma healing, as they activate the parasympathetic nervous system, promoting relaxation and a sense of safety.

Tai chi, a Chinese martial art known for its slow, flowing movements, is another body-oriented intervention that can support trauma healing. Tai chi combines breath control, meditation, and gentle movements to promote balance, relaxation, and body awareness. Like yoga, the slow and deliberate movements in tai chi can help regulate the nervous system, reduce anxiety and stress, and promote a sense of embodiment and grounding.

These body-oriented interventions provide individuals with tools and practices to regulate their bodies and promote a sense of safety and well-being. By engaging in these practices, individuals can gain a greater understanding of their body's responses to trauma, release stored tension and emotions, and promote healing and integration on a physical, emotional, and psychological level.

It is important to work with trauma-informed instructors or therapists experienced in these practices to ensure a safe and supportive environment that respects boundaries and provides appropriate guidance and modifications based on individual needs and capacities. These interventions should be approached with sensitivity and tailored to each person's unique healing journey.

5.5 Touch and Somatic Touch Psychotherapy

Touch and somatic touch psychotherapy are therapeutic approaches that involve the intentional use of touch as part of trauma healing and recovery. These approaches recognize the profound impact that touch can have on the body and mind and aim to support individuals in reconnecting with their bodies, establishing safety, and healing from traumatic experiences.

In somatic touch psychotherapy, trained practitioners use various forms of touch to facilitate the therapeutic process. This can include gentle touch, supportive touch, or more targeted touch-based techniques, depending on the needs and preferences of the individual. The touch is applied with the client's consent and within clear boundaries established through informed consent and ongoing communication.

The use of touch in trauma therapy can have several therapeutic benefits. It can help individuals develop a felt sense of safety, connection, and embodiment, which may have been compromised due to traumatic experiences. Touch can also support the regulation of the nervous system, helping individuals to self-soothe and manage overwhelming emotions.

It's essential to note that touch in trauma therapy is highly specialized and requires extensive training, ethical considerations, and a deep understanding of trauma-informed principles. Practitioners who incorporate touch into their work with trauma survivors should have appropriate qualifications, adhere to professional guidelines and ethical codes, and prioritize the safety and consent of their clients.

However, it's important to acknowledge that touch may not be appropriate or desired for all individuals or in all therapeutic contexts. Trauma survivors may have unique sensitivities, boundaries, or histories that make touch uncomfortable or triggering. Therefore, consent and clear communication play a fundamental role in ensuring that touch is used in a safe and supportive manner.

Practitioners who use touch as part of trauma therapy should always prioritize the empowerment and autonomy of clients, creating a safe and trusting environment where individuals can communicate their preferences and boundaries freely. Clients should have the option to decline or modify touch-based interventions, and their comfort and consent should be continuously respected.

It is crucial for individuals seeking trauma therapy to engage with therapists who have specific training and experience in touch-based approaches and who adhere to appropriate professional and ethical guidelines. Practitioners who incorporate touch in trauma therapy will prioritize the well-being and safety of their clients, creating a space where touch can contribute positively to the healing process.

5.6 Resourcing and Self-Regulation Techniques

Resourcing and self-regulation techniques are essential tools in trauma therapy that help individuals regulate their nervous system, build resilience, and create a sense of safety and stability in the face of traumatic experiences. These techniques enable individuals to access internal and external resources that support their healing and promote self-care.

Resourcing involves identifying and cultivating internal and external resources that individuals can draw upon for support during times of distress or activation. Internal resources can include strengths, positive memories, skills, or qualities that individuals possess, such as resilience, creativity, or a sense of humor. External resources can include supportive relationships, safe environments, or grounding objects that provide comfort and stability.

In therapy, resourcing can be done through various techniques, such as guided imagery, visualizations, or creating resource cards or lists. These techniques help individuals connect with their internal and external resources, reinforcing a sense of safety, grounding, and empowerment. Resourcing can be particularly helpful in managing distressing emotions, reducing the intensity of traumatic memories or triggers, and promoting emotional regulation.

Self-regulation techniques involve practices that individuals can engage in to effectively manage their physiological arousal and emotional states. These techniques help individuals bring their nervous system into balance, promoting a sense of calmness and control in the face of trauma-related triggers or stress.

Some common self-regulation techniques for trauma include:

1. Deep breathing: Practicing deep, diaphragmatic breathing helps activate the body's relaxation response by slowing down the heart rate and calming the nervous system.

2. Grounding exercises: Grounding techniques, such as sensory grounding or body scans, help individuals bring their attention to the present moment and their immediate surroundings, providing a sense of safety and stability.

3. Self-soothing techniques: Engaging in activities that provide comfort and relaxation, such as taking a warm bath, listening to soothing music, or engaging in a favorite hobby, can help individuals self-soothe and regulate their emotions.

4. Mindfulness and meditation: Practicing mindfulness involves intentionally paying attention to the present moment without judgment. Mindfulness-based techniques and meditation can help individuals cultivate awareness, reduce anxiety, and enhance emotional regulation.

5. Movement and exercise: Engaging in gentle movement or exercise, such as yoga, dancing, or walking, can promote physical and emotional well-being, release tension from the body, and regulate the nervous system.

6. Self-care practices: Prioritizing self-care activities, such as getting enough sleep, maintaining a balanced diet, practicing good hygiene, and nurturing healthy relationships, supports overall well-being and resilience in the face of trauma.

It's important to note that self-regulation techniques may vary from person to person, and it's essential to find the techniques that work best for each individual. Therapists trained in trauma-informed approaches can provide guidance and support in identifying and practicing effective self-regulation techniques.

Building resourcing and self-regulation skills takes time and practice, and it may be beneficial for individuals to work with a therapist or counselor to develop and refine these techniques. With consistent use, resourcing and self-regulation techniques can become valuable tools for individuals to manage the impact of trauma, enhance their well-being, and promote healing and recovery.

Working with Traumatic Memories and Triggers

Working with traumatic memories and triggers is an essential aspect of healing and recovery for individuals who have experienced trauma. Traumatic memories can often elicit intense emotional and physical reactions, while triggers can bring about a sense of fear, panic, or distress. Addressing and processing these memories and triggers is crucial in reducing their impact and promoting healing. Through various therapeutic approaches, such as trauma-focused therapies, mindfulness techniques, gradual exposure, and self-care strategies, individuals can learn to navigate and manage their traumatic experiences in a safe and supportive manner. Working with traumatic memories and triggers requires a compassionate and skilled approach, which can be facilitated by a mental health professional trained in trauma therapy.

6.1 Trauma Processing and Integration

Trauma processing and integration is a therapeutic process that focuses on addressing and resolving traumatic memories, emotions, and beliefs. The goal is to help individuals make sense of their traumatic experiences, reduce distressing symptoms, and integrate the fragmented aspects of their identity that may have been disrupted by the trauma.

Trauma processing typically involves several key components:

1. Creating safety: Establishing a safe and supportive therapeutic environment is crucial for trauma processing. This includes building trust between the individual and the therapist, ensuring physical and emotional safety, and providing a non-judgmental space for the individual to express their experiences and emotions.

2. Establishing stabilization: Before delving into traumatic memories, it is important to ensure that the individual has developed effective coping skills and emotional regulation strategies to manage distress. This may involve learning relaxation techniques, grounding exercises, and developing healthy self-care routines.

3. Trauma narrative: Sharing the trauma story in a structured and systematic manner helps individuals gain a sense of mastery and control over their experiences. This may involve recounting the details of the traumatic event, exploring associated thoughts and beliefs, and expressing the emotions that arise.

4. Processing emotions and cognitions: Through various therapeutic techniques, such as cognitive restructuring, EMDR, or imaginal exposure, individuals can work through the intense emotions and negative beliefs associated with the trauma. This involves challenging distorted thoughts, reframing beliefs, and allowing for the processing and release of suppressed emotions.

5. Integration and meaning-making: As the traumatic memories are processed and the associated emotions are addressed, the individual can begin to integrate the traumatic experience into their broader life narrative. This process involves making sense of the trauma, finding meaning or lessons learned, and reclaiming a sense of identity that incorporates the trauma without being defined by it.

6. Gradual exposure and reprocessing: Over time, individuals may engage in gradual exposure to triggers or reminders of the trauma to build resilience and reduce reactivity. This exposure is done in a controlled and supportive way, allowing for reprocessing of the triggers and integration of new, adaptive responses.

Trauma processing and integration can be a challenging and complex journey. It is important to work with a skilled and compassionate mental health professional who specializes in trauma therapy to guide and support individuals through this process. The aim is to not only alleviate the distress caused by traumatic experiences but to empower individuals to move forward in their lives with a renewed sense of strength, resilience, and healing.

6.2 EMDR and Bilateral Stimulation

EMDR (Eye Movement Desensitization and Reprocessing) is a psychotherapy approach that was initially developed to help individuals process traumatic memories and alleviate distressing symptoms associated with trauma. One of the key components of EMDR is bilateral stimulation.

Bilateral stimulation refers to the rhythmic and alternating stimulation of the brain's hemispheres, typically done through eye movements, sounds, or physical sensations. During an EMDR session, the therapist guides the individual to focus on specific traumatic memories or distressing thoughts while simultaneously engaging in bilateral stimulation.

The bilateral stimulation is believed to facilitate the integration of traumatic memories into a more adaptive and less distressing form. This process is thought to occur by activating and accessing different areas of the brain, promoting the reprocessing of the traumatic memory and associated negative emotions and beliefs.

The specific mode of bilateral stimulation can vary depending on the individual's preference and therapeutic approach. Commonly, eye movements are used, where the individual follows the therapist's back-and-forth hand movements. However, other methods such as auditory tones or tapping sensations may be employed.

The bilateral stimulation in EMDR aims to replicate the natural brain processing that occurs during Rapid Eye Movement (REM) sleep, which is believed to play a role in emotional memory consolidation. By engaging in the rhythmic and bilateral stimulation, individuals may experience a decrease in the intensity and distress associated with traumatic memories.

It's important to note that the exact mechanisms of how EMDR and bilateral stimulation work are still being researched and understood. However, numerous studies have demonstrated the effectiveness of EMDR in reducing symptoms of trauma, such as flashbacks, nightmares, and anxiety.

EMDR is typically delivered in a structured manner, involving several phases that include preparation, assessment, desensitization, installation of positive beliefs, and closure. The bilateral stimulation is utilized during the desensitization phase to facilitate the processing and reintegration of traumatic memories.

It's essential to work with a trained and qualified EMDR therapist who can guide and support individuals through the process. EMDR can be an effective treatment approach for a range of traumatic experiences but may not be suitable for everyone. It's always recommended to discuss the appropriateness of EMDR with a mental health professional to determine the most suitable therapy for an individual's specific needs.

6.3 Body Memory and Somatic Resonance

Body memory refers to the concept that the body retains memories of past experiences, including traumatic events, even if they are not consciously remembered. These memories are stored in the body at a sensory and physiological level, and they can influence a person's emotions, physical sensations, and behaviors.

When a person experiences trauma, the body's physiological responses become activated for survival purposes. These responses include increased heart rate, elevated cortisol levels, and tense muscles. Over time, these physiological responses can become ingrained in the body's memory, leading to ongoing physical symptoms and reactions even after the traumatic event has passed.

Somatic resonance, on the other hand, refers to the phenomenon where individuals can resonate with and experience sensations, emotions, or reactions similar to those of another person or a collective group. It is as if their bodies "pick up" the energetic or vibrational frequencies from others and mirror them.

In the context of trauma, somatic resonance can occur when individuals are exposed to the stories or experiences of others who have lived through traumatic events. They may feel sensations or emotions that mirror those of the person sharing their trauma, even if they have not directly experienced a similar event themselves. This resonance can happen through empathetic attunement, mirroring, or a somatic understanding of another person's experience.

Both body memory and somatic resonance highlight the interconnectedness of the mind and body. They emphasize that trauma is not merely a psychological phenomenon but also deeply embedded in our physical being. Recognizing and addressing these aspects is important in trauma healing and recovery.

Therapeutic approaches that focus on the body, such as somatic experiencing, sensorimotor psychotherapy, or body-oriented therapies, can be particularly beneficial in working with body memory and somatic resonance. These approaches explore the physical sensations, movements, and patterns of the body to release and integrate the stored traumatic experiences, facilitate healing, and restore a sense of safety and embodiment.

By bringing awareness to the body's responses and engaging in somatic practices, individuals can learn to regulate their nervous system, release tension and stored trauma, and develop a greater sense of connection with themselves and others.

It's important to work with a skilled and trauma-informed therapist who understands the significance of body memory and somatic resonance in the healing process. They can provide guidance and support to help individuals navigate these experiences and work towards resolution and integration.

6.4 Working with Flashbacks and Dissociation

Working with flashbacks and dissociation involves addressing and mitigating the distressing symptoms associated with trauma. Flashbacks are intrusive and vivid re-experiences of past traumatic events, while dissociation is a state of disconnection from oneself or the surrounding reality, often as a coping mechanism to protect against overwhelming emotions.

Here are some approaches to working with flashbacks and dissociation:

1. Psychoeducation: Educating individuals about the nature of flashbacks and dissociation can help normalize their experiences and provide validation. Understanding that these responses are common reactions to trauma can reduce feelings of shame or confusion.

2. Grounding techniques: Grounding techniques help individuals reorient themselves to the present moment when they experience a flashback or dissociative episode. This can involve focusing on sensory experiences, such as feeling the ground beneath their feet, listening to sounds in the environment, or touching objects around them.

3. Emotional regulation: Developing skills to regulate emotions can be crucial in managing the overwhelming emotions often associated with flashbacks and dissociation. This can involve deep breathing exercises, progressive

muscle relaxation, or engaging in activities that promote relaxation and self-soothing.

4. Creating a safe space: Establishing a sense of safety is vital when working with flashbacks and dissociation. This can include creating a safe and supportive therapeutic environment, where individuals feel comfortable expressing their experiences without judgment or retraumatization. Building trust and rapport with a therapist is essential in creating this safe space.

5. Trauma-focused therapy: Therapeutic approaches such as Eye Movement Desensitization and Reprocessing (EMDR), Cognitive Processing Therapy (CPT), or Dialectical Behavior Therapy (DBT) can effectively address flashbacks and dissociation. These therapies help individuals process traumatic memories, reframe negative beliefs, and develop coping skills to manage distressing symptoms.

6. Internal communication and grounding anchors: Encouraging internal communication among different parts or aspects of the self can help individuals navigate flashbacks and dissociation. This can involve identifying grounding anchors, such as safe places or objects, to bring a sense of stability and connection during disorienting experiences.

7. Self-care and self-compassion: Practicing self-care routines and cultivating self-compassion are essential in managing flashbacks and dissociation. Engaging in activities that promote relaxation, seeking support from loved ones, and practicing self-compassionate thoughts and behaviors can help individuals navigate the challenges associated with these symptoms.

It's important to work with a qualified mental health professional experienced in trauma therapy to support individuals in working through flashbacks and dissociation. The therapist can tailor the approach to the individual's specific needs and provide guidance and support throughout the healing process.

6.5 Enhancing Emotional Awareness and Expression

Enhancing emotional awareness and expression involves developing a deeper understanding of one's emotions and finding healthy ways to express and communicate them. This process allows individuals to cultivate a more authentic and balanced emotional life, leading to improved emotional well-being and the ability to navigate relationships and challenges more effectively.

Here are some strategies for enhancing emotional awareness and expression:

1. Mindfulness: Mindfulness practices, such as meditation, can help individuals develop a more present and non-judgmental awareness of their emotions. By intentionally observing and acknowledging emotions as they arise, individuals can cultivate a greater understanding of their emotional landscape.

2. Emotion labeling: Giving names to emotions as they arise can help individuals recognize and differentiate between different emotions. This can be as simple as saying "I'm feeling sad," "I'm feeling anxious," or "I'm feeling excited." Labeling emotions can enhance self-awareness and facilitate effective expression.

3. Journaling: Writing in a journal can be a powerful tool for exploring and expressing emotions. It provides a safe and private space to freely express thoughts and feelings. Journaling allows individuals to reflect on their experiences,

identify patterns, and gain insight into their emotional responses.

4. Artistic and creative expression: Engaging in artistic or creative outlets, such as drawing, painting, writing poetry, or playing music, can offer alternative ways to express and process emotions. These activities provide a non-verbal language for emotional expression, allowing for a deeper exploration and release of emotions.

5. Seeking support: Sharing emotions and seeking support from trusted individuals can be invaluable in enhancing emotional awareness and expression. This could involve talking to a close friend, family member, or therapist who can provide a safe and non-judgmental space to discuss emotions openly.

6. Emotional regulation techniques: Learning effective strategies to regulate and manage emotions can help individuals express their emotions in healthy ways. These techniques may include deep breathing exercises, practicing self-care activities, engaging in physical exercise, or seeking professional support when needed.

7. Empathy and perspective-taking: Developing empathy and the ability to understand others' emotions can enhance emotional awareness and expression. By considering the emotions and perspectives of others, individuals can gain insight into their own emotional experiences and find more effective ways to communicate and connect with others.

Enhancing emotional awareness and expression is a personal and ongoing process. It involves gentle self-reflection, practice, and a willingness to explore and embrace the rich tapestry of emotions that make up our human experience. Working with a therapist or counselor skilled in emotion-focused approaches can provide additional support and guidance in this journey.

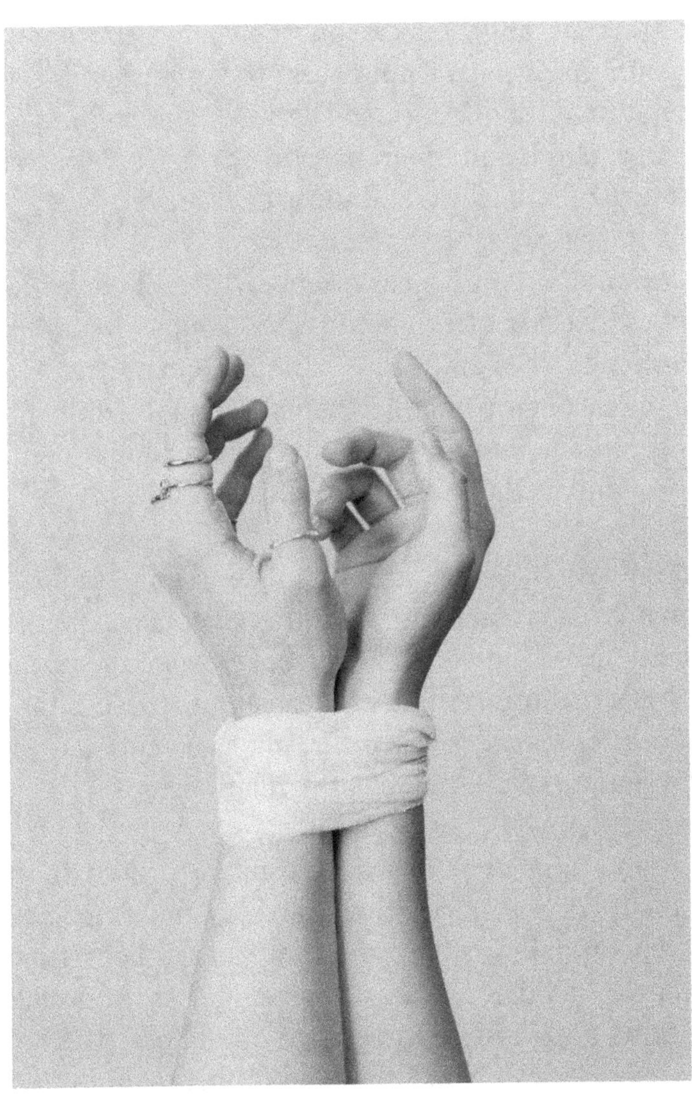

Trauma and Attachment

Trauma and attachment are two interrelated concepts that significantly influence a person's psychological and emotional well-being. Trauma refers to experiences that overwhelm an individual's ability to cope and can lead to long-lasting negative effects on their physical, emotional, and mental health. Attachment, on the other hand, refers to the emotional bond formed between individuals, often between a child and their primary caregiver, that shapes their future relationships and sense of security.

When traumatic experiences occur early in life or within the context of insecure attachment relationships, the impact can be particularly significant. Trauma can disrupt the development of secure attachment, leading to difficulties in forming and maintaining healthy relationships, regulating emotions, and feeling safe in the world.

Understanding the connection between trauma and attachment is crucial in providing effective support and intervention for individuals who have experienced trauma. By addressing both trauma and attachment issues together, individuals can work towards healing the emotional wounds and developing secure and healthy relationships.

Therapeutic approaches such as trauma-focused therapies, attachment-based interventions, and trauma-informed care can help individuals explore and heal their traumatic experiences while also addressing any attachment disruptions or insecurities. By providing a safe and supportive environment, these approaches aim to foster secure attachment and promote resilience and well-being.

7.1 Understanding the Impact of Trauma on Attachment

The impact of trauma on attachment can be profound and far-reaching. Traumatic experiences can disrupt the development of secure attachment, which is the foundation for healthy and trusting relationships. Here are some key ways in which trauma can influence attachment:

1. Insecure attachment styles: Trauma can lead to the development of insecure attachment styles, such as anxious, avoidant, or disorganized attachment. These attachment styles often involve difficulties in trusting others, establishing emotional closeness, or maintaining a sense of safety in relationships.

2. Hyperarousal and hypervigilance: Trauma can result in heightened states of arousal and hypervigilance, making it challenging for individuals to feel safe around others. This can lead to difficulties forming secure attachments and establishing a sense of trust.

3. Fear of intimacy and closeness: Traumatic experiences can create a fear of intimacy and emotional closeness due to the association of relationships with danger or harm. Individuals may struggle with allowing themselves to be vulnerable and may distance themselves from others as a protective mechanism.

4. Internal working models: Trauma can shape an individual's internal working models of relationships, which are cognitive representations of how relationships and

interactions are expected to unfold. These internal models can be influenced by past traumatic experiences, leading to negative expectations of others, mistrust, and difficulty forming healthy attachments.

5. Complex trauma and attachment disruptions: Complex trauma, which involves prolonged or repeated trauma experienced within relationships, can have a particularly profound impact on attachment. It can disrupt the ability to form secure attachments, leading to difficulties with emotional regulation, self-identity, and maintaining stable relationships.

6. Transgenerational transmission: Trauma can be transmitted across generations as unresolved trauma and attachment disruptions can impact how individuals interact with their own children. Unresolved trauma can affect parenting styles, attachment patterns, and the ability to provide a secure base for their children.

Understanding the impact of trauma on attachment is crucial for providing appropriate support and intervention. Therapies that address both trauma and attachment, such as trauma-focused therapy and attachment-based interventions, can help individuals heal from the effects of trauma, build secure attachments, and develop healthier relational patterns. It's important to work with a qualified and experienced mental health professional who specializes in trauma and attachment to guide this healing process.

7.2 Repairing Attachment Wounds through Somatic Approaches

Repairing attachment wounds through somatic approaches involves addressing the trauma that occurs within the body as a result of disrupted or unhealthy attachment relationships. Somatic approaches focus on the body's role in processing and healing trauma, recognizing that trauma is stored not only in the mind, but also in the physical sensations, movements, and functions of the body.

Attachment wounds occur when there is a disruption or absence of secure and healthy attachment relationships in early life. These wounds can result from experiences such as neglect, abuse, or inconsistent caregiving. They can negatively impact a person's ability to form and maintain healthy relationships throughout their lives, leading to difficulties with trust, intimacy, and emotional regulation.

Somatic approaches to repairing attachment wounds aim to address the underlying physical and emotional imprints of trauma in the body. These approaches draw from various modalities, including Somatic Experiencing, Sensorimotor Psychotherapy, and Body-Oriented Psychotherapy, among others. They recognize that the body holds valuable information about a person's history, and that by bringing awareness to the body, healing can occur.

One key aspect of somatic approaches is helping individuals develop a greater awareness of their body sensations, movements, and internal experiences. This can involve practices such as mindfulness, grounding exercises, and body scans to help individuals become more attuned to their bodily experiences. By cultivating this awareness, individuals can begin to notice patterns and triggers that may be linked to their attachment wounds.

Another important aspect of somatic approaches is working with the body to process and release trauma. Trauma is often held in the body as frozen or stuck energy. Somatic therapy techniques such as gentle movement, breathwork, and touch can help individuals safely release and discharge this energy. By allowing the body to move and express itself, individuals can begin to release the stored trauma and create space for healing.

Additionally, somatic approaches focus on restoring a sense of safety and regulation within the body. This can involve practices such as grounding exercises, self-soothing techniques, and creating a felt sense of safety through touch or body awareness. By helping individuals regulate their nervous system and feel safe within their bodies, somatic approaches support the healing of attachment wounds.

It is important to note that repairing attachment wounds through somatic approaches is a process that takes time and patience. It requires a skilled and attuned therapist who can support individuals in exploring their bodily experiences in a safe and supportive environment. As individuals engage in somatic therapy, they can gradually begin to rebuild their capacity for secure attachment, develop healthier relationship patterns, and experience increased resilience and well-being.

In conclusion, repairing attachment wounds through somatic approaches recognizes the integral role of the body in healing trauma and restoring healthy attachment patterns. By attuning to the body's sensations, movements, and internal experiences, individuals can begin to process and release stored trauma. Through practices that promote safety and regulation, individuals can develop a sense of security within their bodies and work towards establishing healthier attachment relationships. With time and professional support, somatic approaches can help individuals repair attachment wounds and experience greater well-being.

7.3 Polyvagal-informed Interventions for Enhancing Attachment

Polyvagal-informed interventions for enhancing attachment refer to therapeutic approaches that are based on the understanding of the polyvagal theory, which explores the intricate relationship between the autonomic nervous system, social engagement, and attachment. The polyvagal theory, developed by Dr. Stephen Porges, highlights the role of the vagus nerve in regulating our social behaviors and responses to stress and threat.

Polyvagal-informed interventions focus on regulating the autonomic nervous system, promoting feelings of safety and connection, and supporting the development of secure attachment relationships. These interventions can be helpful for individuals who have experienced attachment wounds and struggle with forming and maintaining healthy relationships.

One key aspect of polyvagal-informed interventions is working with the nervous system to regulate states of arousal. The polyvagal theory recognizes three distinct states: the ventral vagal state, associated with feelings of safety and social engagement; the sympathetic state, associated with fight-or-flight responses; and the dorsal vagal state, associated with freeze and dissociation responses.

Polyvagal-informed interventions aim to help individuals restore balance and access the ventral vagal state, where healthy attachments can occur. This can involve practices such as deep breathing, grounding exercises, and self-regulation techniques that promote a sense of safety and calm . By supporting individuals in regulating their nervous system, these interventions create a foundation for building secure attachment relationships.

Another important aspect of polyvagal-informed interventions is promoting social engagement and connection. The polyvagal theory emphasizes the role of facial expressions, vocal prosody, and other non-verbal cues in fostering social engagement. Interventions that incorporate these elements can help individuals feel seen, heard, and understood, which is vital for developing healthy attachment bonds.

Polyvagal-informed interventions may include activities such as attuned listening, mirroring, or collaborative play. These activities aim to create a safe and attuned therapeutic environment where individuals can experience and practice healthy attachment behaviors. By fostering positive social interactions, these interventions support the development of secure attachment and interpersonal skills.

Furthermore, polyvagal-informed interventions address the impact of trauma on the nervous system and attachment patterns. Trauma can disrupt the autonomic nervous system and create dysregulation, making it challenging for individuals to engage in healthy attachment behaviors. These interventions focus on helping individuals process and integrate their traumatic experiences, promoting healing and creating space for healthier attachment patterns to develop.

It is important to note that polyvagal-informed interventions should be conducted by therapists who have a deep understanding of the polyvagal theory and are trained in supporting attachment healing. This ensures that interventions are tailored to the unique needs and experiences of each individual.

In conclusion, polyvagal-informed interventions for enhancing attachment focus on regulating the autonomic nervous system, promoting social engagement, and addressing the impact of trauma on attachment patterns. By creating a sense of safety, fostering positive social interactions, and supporting trauma healing, these interventions help individuals develop and maintain healthy attachment relationships. Polyvagal-informed approaches provide a valuable framework for understanding and addressing attachment wounds, and can be powerful tools for promoting resilience and well-being.

Cultural Considerations in Somatic Trauma Healing

Cultural considerations in somatic trauma healing recognize the significant influence of cultural context on an individual's experience of trauma and their healing process. It acknowledges that trauma is not a universal experience, but is shaped by societal norms, values, and beliefs. Cultural considerations in somatic trauma healing emphasize the importance of honoring and integrating cultural identities, practices, and understandings of healing in the therapeutic process. By incorporating a culturally sensitive approach, trauma healing can become more inclusive, respectful, and effective for individuals from diverse cultural backgrounds.

8.1 Cultural Sensitivity and Responsiveness

Cultural sensitivity and responsiveness in trauma refers to the understanding and acknowledgement of the impact of culture on an individual's experience of trauma, as well as the incorporation of culturally appropriate and relevant approaches in trauma healing.

Cultural sensitivity involves recognizing and respecting the diversity of cultural backgrounds, beliefs, values, and practices that individuals bring to the healing process. It requires therapists to approach trauma with an open mind, free from assumptions or judgments about cultural norms and expectations. By being culturally sensitive, therapists can create a safe and inclusive space for individuals to share their experiences and seek support.

Cultural responsiveness takes cultural sensitivity a step further by actively incorporating culturally appropriate approaches into trauma healing. This involves understanding and respecting the unique ways that different cultures understand and respond to trauma and incorporating those perspectives into therapeutic interventions. It also requires therapists to be aware of potential cultural barriers or biases that may impact the healing process and adapting their approach accordingly.

Culturally sensitive and responsive trauma healing acknowledges that cultural factors can shape how trauma is experienced, expressed, and healed. It recognizes that certain cultural groups may have unique coping mechanisms, healing practices, or cultural ceremonies that can be integrated into the therapeutic process. By incorporating these cultural elements, individuals are more likely to feel understood, validated, and supported in their healing journey. It is important to note that cultural sensitivity and responsiveness should be consistently practiced throughout the entire trauma healing process, from initial assessment and treatment planning to ongoing support and aftercare. Therapists should continuously educate themselves about cultural differences and seek supervision or consultation when necessary to ensure that they are providing the most effective and appropriate care.

In conclusion, cultural sensitivity and responsiveness in trauma recognizes and values the influence of culture on an individual's experience of trauma and their healing journey. By being aware of and incorporating culturally appropriate approaches, therapists can create a safe and inclusive space where individuals from diverse cultural backgrounds can heal and recover from trauma in a way that is respectful and relevant to their unique cultural context.

8.2 Trauma Healing Across Different Cultural Contexts

Trauma healing across different cultural contexts is a complex and nuanced process that requires an understanding and appreciation of the diverse cultural beliefs, practices, and values that shape individuals' experiences and perceptions of trauma. It recognizes that trauma is not a universal experience, but is influenced by cultural contexts and social systems.

When working with trauma in different cultural contexts, it is crucial to approach the healing process with cultural humility, which involves acknowledging the limitations of our own perspectives and actively seeking to understand and respect the cultural background and context of the individuals we are working with.

One important aspect of trauma healing across different cultural contexts is recognizing and validating the unique ways in which trauma is conceptualized and experienced. Each culture may have its own language, cultural symbols, and belief systems that inform how trauma is understood and processed. It is important for the therapist to listen and learn from the individual, allowing them to express their experiences and beliefs without judgement or imposing their own cultural framework.

Additionally, cultural traditions, ceremonies, and healing practices may play a significant role in trauma healing within specific cultural contexts. These practices can include rituals, storytelling, dance, art, or traditional medicine. Integrating and honoring these practices can facilitate healing and empowerment for individuals within their cultural context.

Building trust and establishing rapport is essential when working across different cultural contexts. It is important for therapists to engage in cultural sensitivity and responsiveness, actively learning about the cultural norms, values, and traditions of the individuals they are working with. This may involve seeking consultation from cultural experts or community leaders, and engaging in ongoing education and self-reflection to expand cultural competence.

Cultural considerations in trauma healing also involve acknowledging and addressing systemic and structural factors that contribute to or perpetuate trauma within specific cultural contexts. This can include exploring power dynamics, historical trauma, and social inequalities that may impact an individual's experience and recovery from trauma. It is important for therapists to advocate for systemic changes and provide support that empowers individuals to address the broader cultural and social factors that contribute to trauma.

Ultimately, trauma healing across different cultural contexts requires therapists to approach their work with sensitivity, respect, and an open mind to the diverse ways in which trauma is experienced, understood, and healed within each cultural context. It is through collaboration, cultural humility, and a commitment to learning and adapting that trauma healing can be effective and empowering for individuals across diverse cultural backgrounds.

8.3 Intersectionality and Trauma Recovery

Intersectionality refers to the interconnected nature of social identities, such as race, gender, class, sexuality, and ability, and how they overlap and interact to shape an individual's experiences and identities. When applied to trauma recovery, intersectionality acknowledges that individuals may experience multiple forms of oppression and discrimination, which can compound the impact of trauma and influence the healing process.

Trauma recovery through an intersectional lens recognizes that the experiences and needs of marginalized individuals, who may face intersecting systems of oppression, should be addressed in a comprehensive and inclusive way. It highlights the importance of understanding the ways in which various forms of identity and social categories intersect to affect an individual's vulnerability to trauma, access to resources, and experiences of recovery.

For example, a survivor of sexual assault who is also a racial minority and economically disadvantaged may face additional barriers to recovery due to systemic racism, poverty, and lack of access to culturally competent support services. Intersectionality helps us understand that trauma recovery should not be approached as a one-size-fits-all solution, but rather requires an understanding of the unique and complex intersections of an individual's social identities and experiences of oppression.

In trauma recovery, intersectionality calls for the integration of culturally responsive practices and an understanding of the ways in which systems of power and privilege intersect to impact an individual's experience of trauma and recovery. This may include providing support that addresses structural barriers, engaging in advocacy efforts for social change, and addressing the unique needs and experiences of individuals with multiple marginalized identities.

Trauma recovery through an intersectional lens also emphasizes the importance of centering the voices and experiences of marginalized individuals in their own healing journey. This involves creating spaces that are inclusive, validating, and affirming of diverse identities and perspectives. It also involves recognizing and challenging the ways in which systems of power and privilege can perpetuate trauma and hinder recovery.

In conclusion, intersectionality in trauma recovery recognizes that individuals' experiences of trauma are shaped by the intersecting systems of oppression and privilege they navigate. Addressing trauma through an intersectional lens involves understanding and addressing the unique challenges and needs of individuals with multiple marginalized identities. It prioritizes the importance of inclusive, culturally responsive practices and the empowerment of individuals as active agents in their own healing process.

Integration and Continuum of Care

Integration and continuum of care refers to a comprehensive and cohesive approach to healthcare that ensures seamless transitions and continuity of services across different levels and settings of care. It recognizes that individuals may require various types and intensities of care throughout their health journey, and emphasizes the importance of integrating these services to provide holistic and effective support. By promoting collaboration among healthcare providers and creating a unified system of care, integration and continuum of care aims to improve patient outcomes, enhance patient experience, and optimize resource utilization.

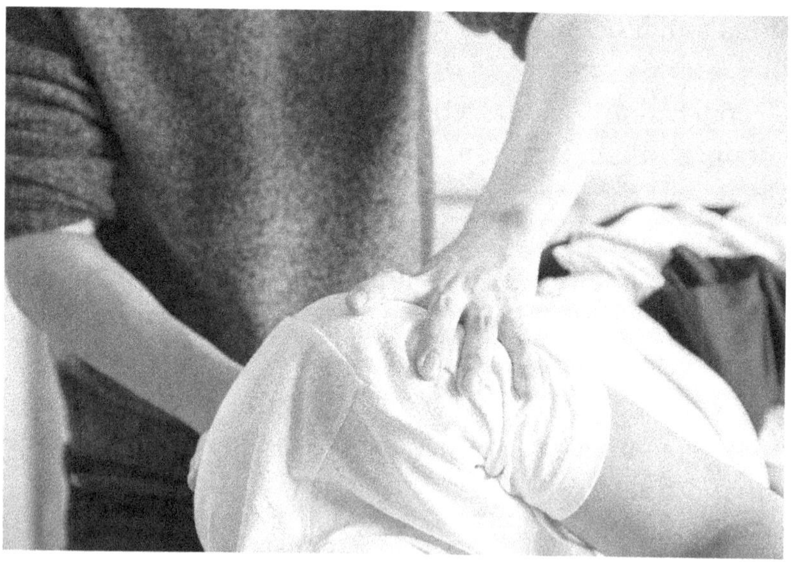

9.1 Integrating Somatic Approaches with Talk Therapy

Integrating somatic approaches with talk therapy involves combining traditional talk therapy techniques with body-based interventions to support a more comprehensive and holistic therapeutic experience. This integration recognizes that the mind and body are intimately connected, and that addressing both aspects can enhance the healing process.

Somatic approaches focus on the body's role in processing and healing trauma, recognizing that trauma is stored not only in the mind, but also in the physical sensations and functions of the body. These approaches may include techniques such as mindfulness, breathwork, movement, and touch, among others, to support individuals in accessing and releasing trauma held in the body.

Talk therapy, on the other hand, primarily focuses on verbal communication and insight-oriented discussions to explore thoughts, emotions, and beliefs related to the trauma. It provides an opportunity for individuals to gain understanding, challenge distorted thinking patterns, and develop healthier coping strategies.

By integrating somatic approaches with talk therapy, therapists can address trauma from both cognitive and physical perspectives, enhancing the healing process. The combination of verbal exploration and body-based interventions can deepen the therapeutic experience, improve emotional regulation, promote grounding and relaxation, and support the integration of traumatic experiences.

This integration allows individuals to gain deeper self-awareness by reconnecting with their bodily sensations, emotions, and physical experiences. It also provides individuals with additional tools and techniques to regulate their nervous system and manage stress and anxiety.

The integration of somatic approaches with talk therapy can be particularly beneficial for individuals who have experienced trauma or have difficulty accessing and expressing their emotions verbally. Somatic approaches can help individuals access and process trauma that may be stored in the body, allowing for a more comprehensive and embodied healing experience.

It is important to note that integrating somatic approaches with talk therapy should be done by therapists who are trained and experienced in both modalities. They should have a deep understanding of trauma and the body's role in healing, as well as the ability to create a safe and supportive therapeutic environment.

In summary, integrating somatic approaches with talk therapy offers a more holistic and comprehensive approach to trauma healing. By addressing the mind and body in therapy, individuals can gain a deeper understanding of their experiences, access and release trauma stored in the body, and develop new strategies for healing and growth.

9.2 Collaborative Care and Multidisciplinary Approach

Collaborative care and a multidisciplinary approach refer to models of healthcare that involve a coordinated and team-based approach to deliver comprehensive and integrated services to individuals. These models recognize that addressing complex healthcare needs requires input from multiple healthcare professionals with diverse areas of expertise.

In collaborative care, healthcare providers work together in a coordinated manner, sharing information, making joint decisions, and actively involving patients in their care. This model promotes effective communication and collaboration between professionals, ensuring that individuals receive the highest level of care by integrating different perspectives and expertise.

A multidisciplinary approach involves assembling a team of healthcare professionals from various disciplines, such as physicians, nurses, psychologists, social workers, and other specialists, to collectively address the diverse needs of patients. Each member of the team contributes their unique knowledge and skills to provide a comprehensive and holistic assessment and treatment plan. The team collaborates to develop individualized care plans, set treatment goals, and regularly review and adjust the plan as needed.

The benefits of collaborative care and a multidisciplinary approach include:

1. Comprehensive assessment: By involving professionals from different disciplines, a broader range of factors can be considered when assessing an individual's health. This can lead to more accurate diagnoses, better understanding of the underlying causes, and more effective treatment planning.

2. Holistic treatment: Collaboration between healthcare professionals ensures that all aspects of a person's health and well-being are considered, including physical, mental, and social factors. This can result in more comprehensive and integrated treatment plans that address the multiple dimensions of a person's health.

3. Enhanced communication and coordination: With collaborative care, healthcare professionals communicate and share information more effectively. This reduces the risk of fragmented care and ensures that all team members are working towards common goals.

4. Improved outcomes: Research has shown that collaborative care and a multidisciplinary approach can lead to improved patient outcomes, including reduced hospital readmissions, improved symptom management, and enhanced overall well-being.

5. Patient-centered care: Collaboration and multidisciplinary approaches prioritize the needs and preferences of individuals. By actively involving patients in their care and considering their unique circumstances and goals, healthcare professionals can provide more personalized and tailored treatment plans.

In summary, collaborative care and a multidisciplinary approach in healthcare involve the integration of various healthcare professionals to provide comprehensive and patient-centered care. This model ensures that individuals receive holistic, coordinated, and effective services across different disciplines, leading to improved outcomes and enhanced overall well-being.

9.3 Supporting Long-Term Healing and Well-being

Supporting long-term healing and well-being refers to providing assistance, resources, and care to individuals who have experienced trauma, illness, or adverse life events. This support aims to help individuals recover physically, mentally, and emotionally, and to establish a sense of overall well-being.

Supporting long-term healing and well-being involves a holistic approach, addressing various aspects of an individual's life. This can include:

1. Physical health: Help individuals access medical care, treatment, and rehabilitation services. Encourage regular exercise, a healthy diet, and adequate sleep to promote physical healing and well-being.

2. Mental health: Provide access to mental health services such as therapy, counseling, or support groups. Help individuals develop coping strategies and resilience to manage stress, anxiety, depression, or other mental health challenges.

3. Emotional support: Offer a safe and empathetic environment for individuals to express their emotions and process their experiences. Encourage healthy emotional expression and provide tools for emotional regulation.

4. Social connections: Facilitate opportunities for individuals to connect with others who can provide support,

understanding, and companionship. This can include friends, family, support groups, or community organizations.

5. Financial stability: Assist individuals in accessing resources and services that can help with financial stability, such as budgeting, job training, education, or social assistance programs. Financial stability is crucial for long-term healing and well-being, as it reduces stress and allows for greater access to necessary resources.

6. Self-care and self-compassion: Promote self-care practices that prioritize individuals' physical, mental, and emotional well-being. Encourage self-compassion by teaching individuals to be kind and understanding toward themselves, and to prioritize their own needs and boundaries.

7. Holistic approaches: Incorporate complementary therapies and practices that promote healing and well-being, such as mindfulness meditation, yoga, art therapy, or nature therapy. These approaches can address the mind-body connection and support overall well-being.

Supporting long-term healing and well-being requires a collaborative approach involving healthcare professionals, mental health providers, social workers, community organizations, and support networks. It is important to tailor support to each individual's unique needs, recognizing that healing and well-being are ongoing processes that may require long-term support.

Ethical Considerations and Self-Care

Ethical considerations and self-care are important concepts that guide our actions and well-being, particularly in fields where we provide care and support to others, such as healthcare, counseling, or social work.

Ethical considerations involve reflecting on the values, principles, and moral obligations that guide our professional conduct. It requires us to make decisions that prioritize the well-being, autonomy, and dignity of the individuals we serve, while also considering the broader social and cultural contexts.

Self-care, on the other hand, involves actively caring for our own physical, mental, and emotional well-being. It is about recognizing our own needs and taking intentional steps to maintain balance, prevent burnout, and foster resilience in our personal and professional lives.

Both ethical considerations and self-care are interconnected. By upholding ethical values and responsibilities, we can provide the best possible care to others, while also ensuring we are not neglecting our own well-being. Prioritizing self-care allows us to sustain our energy, compassion, and effectiveness in our work, while also protecting ourselves from the negative impact of stress and vicarious trauma.

In summary, understanding and integrating ethical considerations and self-care practices are essential for promoting not only the well-being of those we serve but also our own personal and professional fulfillment.

10.1 Ethical Guidelines for Somatic Psychotherapy

Ethical guidelines for somatic psychotherapy provide a framework for ethical and responsible practice in this specific therapeutic approach. Somatic psychotherapy integrates physical, somatic experiences with psychological and emotional processes to promote healing and growth.

Some important ethical guidelines for somatic psychotherapy include:

1. Informed Consent: Obtain informed consent from clients, explaining the nature of somatic psychotherapy, its goals, potential benefits, risks, and limitations. Clients should have a clear understanding of what to expect and have the right to make informed decisions about their participation.

2. Scope of Practice: Ensure that practitioners have appropriate training, education, and expertise in somatic psychotherapy. Practitioners should only provide services within their areas of competence and not engage in practices beyond their training.

3. Confidentiality and Privacy: Respect client confidentiality, privacy, and the ethical duty to protect clients' personal information. Maintain appropriate documentation and handle client records securely and confidentially.

4. Cultural Sensitivity: Respect and be sensitive to clients' diverse cultural backgrounds, beliefs, and values. Take into account cultural factors that may influence somatic

experiences and interpretations, and adapt therapeutic approaches accordingly.

5. Boundaries and Professional Conduct: Maintain clear and appropriate professional boundaries with clients to ensure the therapeutic relationship remains ethical and therapeutic. Avoid dual relationships, conflicts of interest, and exploitation of clients. Refrain from any form of misconduct, such as abuse, harassment, or discrimination.

6. Continuing Education and Supervision: Engage in ongoing professional development, including participating in relevant trainings, workshops, and supervision. Stay informed about current research, best practices, and ethical guidelines in somatic psychotherapy.

7. Client Welfare and Autonomy: Prioritize the well-being and autonomy of clients. Respect their right to make decisions regarding their treatment and involve them in the therapeutic process, including setting goals and determining the pace and duration of therapy.

8. Informed Referrals: If clients require additional or specialized services beyond the scope of somatic psychotherapy, provide informed referrals to appropriate professionals or resources.

9. Regular Self-Care and Professional Support: Engage in regular self-care practices and seek professional support to maintain your own well-being, manage personal issues that may arise during therapy, and prevent burnout or compassion fatigue.

It is important for somatic psychotherapists to adhere to and regularly review these ethical guidelines to ensure responsible, ethical practice, and provide the best possible care for their clients.

10.2 Therapist Self-Care and Vicarious Trauma Prevention

Therapist self-care and vicarious trauma prevention are essential aspects of maintaining the well-being and effectiveness of mental health professionals. Working with clients who have experienced trauma or are dealing with emotional difficulties can be emotionally demanding and may put therapists at risk for vicarious trauma, also known as secondary traumatic stress or compassion fatigue.

Therapist self-care involves actively nurturing and attending to one's own physical, mental, and emotional well-being. It is a proactive approach to managing stress, preventing burnout, and maintaining a healthy work-life balance. Here are some strategies for therapist self-care:

1. Personal Therapy: Engaging in regular therapy can provide therapists with an outlet to process their own feelings, concerns, and challenges in a supportive and confidential environment.

2. Self-Reflection: Practicing regular self-reflection can help therapists recognize and address their own emotions, triggers, and biases that may arise during therapy sessions. This awareness can support more effective self-care and prevent the transfer of personal issues onto clients.

3. Boundaries: Setting clear and appropriate boundaries with clients is crucial for maintaining therapists' emotional well-being and preventing burnout. This includes setting

limits on working hours, caseload, and therapeutic responsibilities.

4. Supportive Networks: Cultivating a network of supportive colleagues, mentors, and friends can provide therapists with an avenue for debriefing, sharing experiences, and seeking guidance. Peer support groups or supervision can also be valuable resources.

5. Self-Care Practices: Engaging in regular self-care activities such as exercise, mindfulness meditation, hobbies, creative expression, or spending time in nature can help therapists relax, recharge, and maintain a sense of personal well-being.

Regarding vicarious trauma prevention, therapists can take specific steps to minimize and manage the impact of absorbing their clients' trauma. Some strategies include:

1. Education and Training: Continuous education and training on vicarious trauma can help therapists understand its signs and symptoms, risk factors, and preventive measures. This knowledge can help therapists recognize when vicarious trauma is emerging and take appropriate action.

2. Self-Awareness: Cultivating self-awareness allows therapists to monitor their emotional and psychological state more effectively. Recognizing signs of vicarious trauma, such as increased emotional sensitivity, fatigue, or cynicism, enables therapists to intervene early and seek support.

3. Self-Regulation Techniques: Learning and practicing techniques for self-regulation can help therapists manage the

emotional intensity experienced during therapy sessions. Deep breathing exercises, grounding techniques, or using sensory-based strategies can help therapists stay present and centered.

4. Peer Support and Supervision: Engaging in regular supervision, consultation, or peer support groups can offer a space for therapists to discuss challenging cases, gain perspective, and receive validation and support from colleagues.

5. Self-Care and Self-Compassion: Prioritizing self-care activities and developing self-compassion practices are crucial for preventing vicarious trauma. Practicing self-care regularly, setting boundaries, and engaging in activities that bring joy and relaxation can help therapists replenish and rejuvenate themselves.

6. Professional Development: Continuing education, attending workshops, and staying up to date with research in trauma and vicarious trauma can enhance therapists' knowledge and skills, allowing them to provide more effective support while minimizing their risk of vicarious trauma.

By implementing therapist self-care and vicarious trauma prevention strategies, mental health professionals can maintain their own well-being and build resilience, enabling them to provide high-quality and compassionate care to their clients.

10.3 Boundaries and Professional Responsibility

Boundaries and professional responsibility are crucial aspects of maintaining ethical and effective practice in various professional roles, including mental health professionals, healthcare providers, and other helping professions.

Boundaries refer to the limits and guidelines that define appropriate and ethical relationships and interactions between professionals and their clients or patients. They help create a safe and therapeutic environment, ensure professional integrity, and protect the well-being and autonomy of clients. Here are some key aspects of boundaries:

1. Emotional Boundaries: Professionals maintain appropriate emotional distance and objectivity, ensuring that their personal emotions and experiences do not interfere with their clients' well-being. They avoid becoming overly involved or dependent on their clients and refrain from sharing their personal problems or seeking emotional support from clients.

2. Physical Boundaries: Professionals maintain appropriate physical distance and contact with clients, ensuring that their interactions are respectful, safe, and within the bounds of professional and ethical norms. They avoid any form of physical contact that is not necessary for therapeutic purposes, and always prioritize the comfort and consent of their clients.

3. Personal and Professional Relationship: Professionals maintain a clear distinction between their personal and professional lives. They avoid dual relationships, such as engaging in social or financial interactions with clients outside of the professional context, to prevent conflicts of interest and maintain objectivity.

4. Confidentiality: Professionals uphold strict confidentiality standards to protect the privacy and sensitive information of their clients. They only disclose client information with consent, when required by law, or when there is a risk of harm to the client or others. They take appropriate measures to secure and protect client records and information.

Professional responsibility encompasses the ethical duties and obligations that professionals have towards their clients, colleagues, profession, and broader society. It involves acting in the best interest of clients, upholding professional standards, and promoting the well-being and integrity of the profession. Here are some key aspects of professional responsibility:

1. Competence and Continuing Education: Professionals strive to maintain and enhance their knowledge, skills, and competence through ongoing learning, professional development, and staying informed about current evidence-based practices in their field.

2. Ethical Conduct: Professionals adhere to a code of ethics or professional standards specific to their field. They engage in ethical decision-making, uphold the values and principles of their profession, and act with integrity, honesty, and respect towards their clients and colleagues.

3. Cultural Sensitivity and Diversity: Professionals are aware of and respect the diversity of their clients, including their cultural backgrounds, beliefs, and values. They employ culturally responsive practices and avoid discrimination or bias based on race, gender, sexual orientation, religion, or any other identity factors.

4. Boundaries with Colleagues: Professionals maintain appropriate boundaries, respect confidentiality, and avoid conflicts of interest in their relationships with colleagues. They collaborate and consult with colleagues when necessary, while respecting their expertise and professional responsibilities.

5. Advocacy and Social Justice: Professionals advocate for the rights and well-being of their clients, working towards equality, social justice, and access to resources and services. They advocate for policies and practices that promote the welfare of their clients and address systemic issues that contribute to inequality and injustice.

6. Duty to Report: Professionals have a duty to report any suspected abuse, neglect, or harm to vulnerable individuals, including children, older adults, or individuals with disabilities, as required by law or professional guidelines.

By establishing and maintaining clear boundaries and fulfilling their professional responsibilities, professionals can ensure the ethical and effective delivery of services, prioritize the well-being of their clients, and contribute to the integrity and reputation of their profession.

Embracing Somatic Psychotherapy as a Path to Healing Trauma

Embracing somatic psychotherapy as a path to healing trauma is a transformative and empowering choice. Trauma affects not only our minds but also our bodies, leaving a profound impact on our overall well-being. Traditional forms of talk therapy may not fully address the somatic manifestations of trauma, and that is where somatic psychotherapy shines.

By recognizing the inherent wisdom of the body and its ability to hold and release trauma, somatic psychotherapy acknowledges that healing happens not just through words but through embodied experiences. This approach invites individuals to explore the language of their bodies, to listen to the messages they hold, and to engage in practices that promote healing and integration.

Somatic psychotherapy offers a range of techniques and interventions that cultivate body awareness, regulation of sensations and emotions, and the rediscovery of safety and empowerment. From gentle body-focused exercises to expressive movement and breathwork, individuals are guided to reconnect with their bodies in a safe and nurturing way. Through this process, they gradually release stored trauma, restore balance, and reclaim agency over their lives.

The beauty of somatic psychotherapy lies in its ability to honor individual experiences and provide a personalized healing journey. Every person's experience of trauma is unique, and somatic approaches recognize and respect these differences. Therapists trained in somatic psychotherapy work collaboratively with individuals, listening to their needs, and tailoring interventions to their specific circumstances.

Moreover, somatic psychotherapy fosters a deep sense of empowerment and resilience. Through this modality, individuals learn to trust their body's innate capacity to heal and regulate itself. They gain tools and strategies that can be incorporated into everyday life, empowering them to navigate future challenges with greater self-awareness and self-care.

Embracing somatic psychotherapy as a path to healing trauma also highlights the importance of the mind-body connection and the interplay between physical and psychological well-being. By addressing both aspects of our being, somatic approaches provide a holistic and comprehensive approach to healing trauma, fostering long-lasting, transformative change.

However, it is essential to recognize that somatic psychotherapy may not be the right fit for everyone. It is crucial for individuals to engage in open and honest discussions with qualified professionals to assess their readiness for this particular approach. Seeking informed consent and collaboration throughout the therapeutic journey is essential to ensure that individuals feel empowered and engaged in their healing process.

In conclusion, embracing somatic psychotherapy provides a powerful and integrative path to healing trauma.

Promoting Resilience and Post-Traumatic Growth

Promoting resilience and post-traumatic growth is a critical aspect of supporting individuals who have experienced trauma or adversity. Resilience refers to an individual's ability to adapt and bounce back from difficult experiences, while post-traumatic growth refers to the positive psychological changes that can emerge in the aftermath of traumatic events.

Promoting resilience involves providing individuals with the necessary tools and resources to cope with adversity and build their capacity to thrive. This can include teaching skills such as problem-solving, emotion regulation, and stress management. Additionally, promoting resilience involves fostering a supportive environment where individuals feel safe, validated, and connected to others.

There are several strategies that can be used to promote resilience and post-traumatic growth. One strategy is to provide individuals with opportunities for self-reflection and self-discovery. This can involve engaging in activities such as journaling, art therapy, or mindfulness practices. By encouraging individuals to reflect on their experiences and explore their emotions, they can gain a deeper understanding of themselves and their capacity for growth.

Another strategy is to encourage individuals to seek out social support. Having a strong support network can provide individuals with the emotional and practical assistance they need to navigate challenging times. This can involve connecting individuals with support groups, counseling services, or other community resources. By fostering a sense of belonging and connection, individuals are more likely to find strength and support in the face of adversity.

Additionally, it is important to promote a sense of optimism and hope. This can be done by highlighting individuals' strengths and accomplishments, and encouraging them to set and work towards meaningful goals. By focusing on the possibilities for growth and positive change, individuals can develop a sense of agency and empowerment.

Lastly, promoting resilience and post-traumatic growth involves creating an environment that allows for ongoing learning and personal development. This can involve providing individuals with opportunities for education and skill-building, as well as facilitating access to resources and information. By encouraging individuals to continue learning and growing, they are better equipped to face future challenges and experiences.

Overall, promoting resilience and post-traumatic growth is a vital aspect of supporting individuals who have experienced trauma or adversity. By providing individuals with the necessary tools, resources, and support, they can develop the capacity to not only survive difficult experiences but thrive in their aftermath.

END